Born in the Spirit of Jesus

Richard Reichert

Dubuque, Iowa

Nihil Obstat
Rev. Richard L. Schaefer

Imprimatur
+Most Rev. Daniel W. Kercera
Archbishop of Dubuque
February 11, 1992

The imprimatur is an official declaration that a book or pamphlet is free of doctrinal or moral error. No implication is contained therein that anyone who granted the imprimatur agrees with the contents, opinions, or statements expressed.

Book Team

Publisher—Ernest T. Nedder
Editor—Mary Jo Graham
Art Director—Cathy Frantz
Production Coordinator—Marilyn Rothenberger

Theological Consultants

Rev. David Kasparek—Director of Religious Education with *The Green Bay Plan*, Diocese of Green Bay, Wisconsin.

Rev. Dennis Colter—Loras College, Archdiocese of Dubuque.

Photo Credits

All photos by James L. Shaffer except
p. 10, 21, 30, 33, and 43 by Robert Roethig

ISBN 0-697-17657-6

20 19 18 17

Contents

Future characters of self
caption
boarder
with detail +
large

1 Decide for Yourself

In many primitive societies, it was common to bring children into the adult community at age twelve. They were then treated like adults and were expected to act like adults. Just a century ago few people in America went to school beyond eighth grade. Instead, they would begin working and take on adult responsibilities. Even today, a girl can legally marry at age fourteen in some states.

On many farms, a child will learn to drive a tractor by age nine or ten and by age twelve is able to handle the machinery well enough to work side-by-side with adults. In many of the poor countries of the world, children leave home at about the age of twelve. They are expected to make a living on their own by then.

Children can become adults sooner than we usually think they can.

You, an Adult?

You have already done a lot of growing in your life. Some of it took place with amazing speed. In the first nine months of life, you grew from two tiny cells to become a very complex organism with billions of cells. Within the first year of your life, you learned how to walk. You mastered a language by three. By the time you were eight, you could read, write, and work with numbers. By now, you have learned any number of rather difficult skills such as playing the piano, swimming, bike riding, skiing, or skate boarding. They may seem easy now, but such skills demanded tremendous coordination of many muscles and nerves. Most of this growing happened very naturally. You probably did not even notice it. Now you are entering a new phase of growth, one that marks you as an adult. Your body is developing (or already has) a new and wonderful capacity—the ability to create new human beings.

An animal is considered an adult as soon as it has developed that capacity, and in a biological sense, you too are entering adulthood right now.

You grow faster the first nine months of your life, while in your mother's womb, than at any other time in your life.

If you were born in a different century or in a different culture, you would probably be considered an adult in a social sense, also. But in our society things are different. It's one thing to be physically able to have children and start a family, but it's another thing to be able to feed and care for a family.

Life was simple in primitive times. If you were old enough to hunt, to tend sheep, or plant seeds, you could feed a family. Now it's not that easy. To feed a family requires money. Money comes from jobs, and most jobs require education and special training. The jobs that do not require education usually do not pay enough to feed a family and provide a home, clothing, medical care, and education.

It now costs parents approximately $125,000 to raise a child from infancy to age eighteen.

This means society expects its young people to continue in school even though they are old enough, physically, to start families of their own. It encourages young people to wait until they have enough education and training to care for a family before they marry. Sometimes, this means waiting until they are twenty-five or even older. It also means depending on parents or other adults during most of that time. Even though young people such as yourself become adults somewhere around the age of twelve, they continue to depend on others for another six or eight years—or longer.

Adulthood: A State of Mind

It is necessary for you to continue to depend on your parents throughout your teens and to follow the rules they set down for you during that time. But even though you will not be able to make certain adult decisions for some time yet, it is not necessary for you to remain a child.

You can make a choice. You can consider yourself a child or an adult. Adolescence is what you decide to make it.

Some prefer to spend their teen years as children. Children have their own way of approaching life. For example, children want things right away. They find it very difficult to wait and almost impossible to pass up some immediate pleasure, like candy, so they can eat a good meal later. Children are not really able to be concerned about other persons or think about long-range effects of what they do, and they cannot always recognize danger.

Adolescence—
A period of transition between childhood and adulthood.

Forty-two percent of today's youth watch television more than three hours a day. Do you think that is being very adult?

For all these reasons, parents spend much of their time taking care of their children. Parents impose rules, such as when to go to bed, where to ride the bicycle, how much television to watch and what kind of shows to watch. Because children cannot take care of themselves, they need all these rules and supervision.

Parents will continue—in fact, they must continue—to impose rules and take care of their children until the children begin to act adult. The sooner you decide to think and act adult, the sooner parents and other adults will treat you like one.

What Is Adult?

Too often, young people have the wrong idea about being adult. They think adult means having your own money, being your own boss, being able to drink and smoke, having your own car, going where you want, with whomever you want, when you want. For them, adult means freedom. That is only half of the picture. The other half is that being adult also means responsibility. Responsibility comes first.

The following is a test you can give yourself. Answer each of the questions with one of the following:

a. always

b. most of the time

c. once in a while

d. almost never

_____ 1. Do you take your school work seriously and do things, such as homework, without having to be told?

_____ 2. Do you stay at a task until it is completed, even if it means you must miss out on something you would rather be doing?

_____ 3. Do you try to avoid too much junk food?

_____ 4. Do you think about how something will affect others before you do it?

_____ 5. Do you think about the long-range effects of your present actions?

_____ 6. Do you go against the group when you think what they are doing is wrong?

_____ 7. Do you respect the property of others?

_____ 8. Do you take care of your own things?

_____ 9. Do you think religion now has an important place in your life?

_____ 10. Do you do what you think is right even if your friends might laugh at you or put you down for it?

_____ 11. Do you think about and respect the feelings of others?

_____ 12. Do you take advice from more experienced adults?

_____ 13. Do you seek the advice of more experienced adults?

_____ 14. Do you learn from past mistakes?

_____ 15. Do you feel a responsibility to help out at home in whatever ways you can?

There's nothing tricky about that little test. It should be obvious that the more you do the kinds of things listed, the more adult you have begun to think and act. If you answered "most of the time" to those fifteen questions you are well on your way. If you did not, then you really shouldn't care if people continue to treat you like a child. You are still acting and thinking like one.

Certainly, there is much more to being adult than what is in the list you just read. But it does give you an idea of how true adults think and act.

Spiritual Adulthood—
The capacity to act responsibly and respect the rights of others.

Biological Adulthood—
The capacity to reproduce the species.

Cultural Adulthood—
The capacity to form, feed, and care for a family in the society in which you live.

Why Be an Adult?

You may feel all this talk about you being adult is a put-on. You know there is no way you are able to do many things older adults can do. For one thing, your parents will not let you. For another, you still lack the experience and education needed. That's true, but adulthood is basically a state of mind. It is being willing to assume responsibility for yourself and for your actions. It is being as concerned for others as you are for yourself. If you are capable of that, you are capable of beginning to act adult right now and throughout your teens.

It may be harder in our society to be adult while still in your teens than it was in earlier times, because, in earlier times and in primitive society, the teen years were spent working side by side with other adults. A teen who did not act adult did not eat. It was that simple. People grew up in a hurry. It may be more difficult to be an adult today, but it is still very possible.

But why bother? Why all the rush to be adult?

Being adult is what life is all about. That's why we are here. To refuse to act adult once you can is—to put it plainly—unnatural.

You will hear some teens say, "Look at the mess the adults have made of the world. There is so much war, greed, and poverty. Who wants to be adult if that's how adults act?" The fact is the mess has not been made by adults. It has been made by people who never became adult. The mess was made by grown-up *children*. The mess was made by people who refused to act and think like adults.

"The world is full of problem children—and most of them are over twenty-one years of age."
J. Harold Smith

The world is short on true adults—responsible, concerned people. We have more than our share of grown-up children. That's why the world needs you, the adult you, as soon as possible. Just as important, the Church needs you, the adult you, as soon as possible.

That's the real reason for this course—to prepare you for confirmation. You are needed! The adult you.

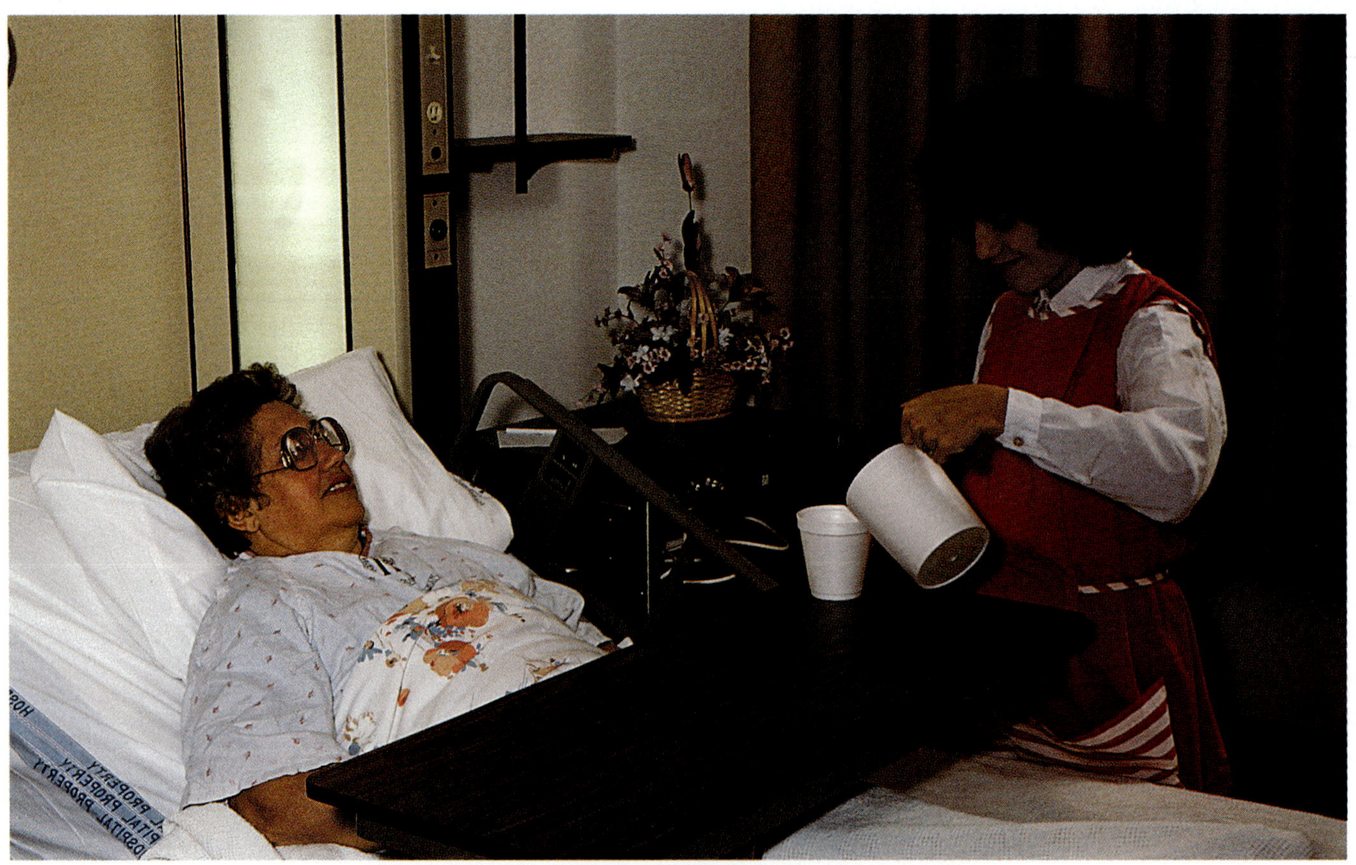

What Is Next?

By the time you enter the teens, you have all the equipment it takes to begin being adult. This means you are capable of assuming responsibility for your own actions, and you have developed an intellect that is able to know right from wrong. All that is left is experience. That takes time—a lifetime. You can keep gathering valuable experience until the day you die. You should never stop growing. There is always more to learn about life. You can always become more adult.

The important thing now is to begin. Being normal, you are going to miss some of the things you must leave behind as you begin to think and act adult. As you struggle to make your first decisions, you will probably miss those childhood days when your parents made all your decisions for you. Being responsible for your own decisions can be scary. You have no one to blame for mistakes but yourself.

It was comfortable being a child. Then it was all right to be self-centered. You didn't have to worry about anything because everyone looked out for you. No one expected you to be concerned about others except in the most simple way. But as an adult, it is not enough to be responsible for yourself alone. You must also become concerned for the good of others. This is a big responsibility and an even bigger challenge that not everyone chooses to accept. Some persons in their teen years and beyond choose to continue to be selfish and irresponsible. They want the freedom of adulthood without its responsibilities. They want it both ways.

God Wants You

As you enter your teen years, there is another big change you are asked to make. There is a child's way to approach God and there is an adult's way. God loved you as a child. Now, God wants to love you as an adult. God also wants you to love Him in an adult way.

God expects you to be adult. He wants you to become a full adult, and a responsible member of His Church. That is no small order. God knows growing up can be hard work; it can be risky, and there will be mistakes. There will be lapses into the old childish ways, once in a while. That's why the Church offers you the Sacrament of Confirmation. We will see just what that means later. For now it is enough to know God reaches out to you and calls you to a new, more adult way of life as you enter your teens. He also helps you make the move.

What is an adult approach to God? This story might help you see:

There was a young Indian brave who came to the chief one day. The brave complained that he was having a hard time finding God. He even doubted that there was a God at all. He asked the chief to help him find God. If the chief couldn't, then the brave said he would no longer follow the religious practices of the tribe. The chief was very understanding. He was also very wise. He asked the brave to come with him down to the river. When they got to the bank of the river, the chief told the brave to place his face just below the surface of the water. The brave gave the chief a puzzled look, but he obeyed. Once he had his face in the river, he let the chief take hold of his shoulders and press him further into the water. At first, the brave thought it was some kind of joke. But the air in his lungs was being used up. He began to try to raise his head from the water. The chief held him down. He struggled, but the chief was too powerful. The brave was almost out of breath. He began to panic. He was now sure the chief was going to kill him for his lack of faith.

He gave one last struggle and fell back, exhausted and breathless. He was about to lose consciousness when the chief finally released him and pulled him from the water. The brave lay gasping for a long time. When he finally regained his breath and his strength, he looked up at the chief. "Why did you do that, sir?" he asked. "I wanted you to help me find God and you almost killed me."

The chief smiled kindly and said, "My son, until every fiber of your being wants to find God the same way your lungs had longed for breath a few moments ago, you won't be looking hard enough for Him."

The moral of the story should be clear. God wants to be taken seriously.

Scripture Search

Read the following passages and be prepared to do these tasks:

1. *Tell the story or main ideas of the passage in your own words.*
2. *Explain how you think the passage relates to the main ideas of this chapter.*
   - *Luke 2:39–52*
   - *Galatians 4: 1–20*
   - *Galatians 5: 13–16*

Summary

There are three kinds of adulthood. When you are physically able to have a baby you are biologically adult. You are culturally adult when you can care for and support a family. You are adult in the spiritual sense when you begin to take personal responsibility for your actions and are willing to respect the rights and needs of others.

Unfortunately, many people who are biologically and culturally adult do not become spiritually adult. Adulthood, therefore, is more a state of mind than a particular age. You have the capacity and are being called to become adult in that spiritual sense. When you become spiritually adult, you begin to form a new, more adult relationship with God.

Chapter 1: Activities

Activity 1

Use a word or phrase to indicate what you feel would be an adult attitude and a childish attitude toward each of the following:

	Adult	**Child**
Clothing	______________	______________
Food	______________	______________
Work	______________	______________
Helping others	______________	______________
Property of others	______________	______________
Being on time	______________	______________
Using time	______________	______________
Religion	______________	______________
Personal health	______________	______________
Education	______________	______________
The future	______________	______________

Activity 2

List what you feel are the five biggest problems or obstacles you and people your age face when trying to act as a responsible adult:

1. ______________________________
2. ______________________________
3. ______________________________
4. ______________________________
5. ______________________________

Compare your list with that of others in your class.
Are the problems you list things you have any control over?
Would you be willing to discuss this list with your parents?
Why or why not?

Activity 3

Make an estimate of what you think your parents will have to spend on you over the next twelve months. If there are four in your family, your share of the expenses would be one-fourth of the total on food, for example.

Food	$ ________
Clothing (include cleaning and washing)	$ ________
Shelter (heat, rent or mortgage, electricity, water, taxes, and so on)	$ ________
Transportation	$ ________
Education (include cost of things such as piano lessons)	$ ________
Entertainment (include things such as family vacations)	$ ________
Medical Health	$ ________
Total	$ ________

If you work and give some of the money earned to your parents, subtract that from the total. Now ask your parents to check your estimates to see how close they are to what your parents actually spend on you.

Activity 4

In the first chapter, we said that God wants to be taken seriously. Just about everyone wants to be taken seriously, except when they are just clowning around. List some of the ways you want to be treated by others when you want to be taken seriously, for example, have others pay attention to what you are saying or doing.

1. ______________________________
2. ______________________________
3. ______________________________
4. ______________________________
5. ______________________________

Using your own list, rank yourself on how seriously you take God. Do you treat God the way you want others to treat you? Circle the number that best says it.

Not at all ______________________ Most of the time

0 1 2 3 4 5 6 7 8 9 10

Choosing a Sponsor

With your parents' help, you are asked to choose a sponsor for your own confirmation. The Church has certain standards a person has to meet before he or she can serve as your sponsor. As you will see, the standards are just common sense. First, your sponsor has to be baptized, be confirmed, and have received the Eucharist. Second, your sponsor has to be at least sixteen years old. (The Church may make exceptions to this rule in very special cases.) Third, your sponsor needs to be a person of faith, that is, a practicing Catholic.

Sponsor—
A person who undertakes the responsibility to guide a confirmation candidate in the preparation for receiving the sacrament. It is the sponsor's role to present the candidate to the Church at the time of the celebration of the sacrament.

I chose ______________________ for my sponsor because:

2 Meeting the Spirit

Newscasters often throw around terms like "a $50 billion budget for defense" or "$10 billion for Medicare." Did you ever try to imagine what a billion dollars actually is? It looks like this: $1,000,000,000. To get some idea of what all those zeros mean, think of this: If someone gave you a million dollars on the condition that you must spend $1000 of it each day until it is all gone, it would take you almost three years to spend it all. If someone gave you a billion dollars with the same conditions, it would take you almost three thousand years to spend it all!

The distances involved in outer space are also difficult to grasp. Take a light year, for example. One of the nearest stars is about ten light years away. Do you know how many miles that is? It's 58.8 trillion miles. This means you could reach that star in ten years—if you could travel at the rate of 186,300 miles per second for each second of those ten years. There are stars hundreds of light years away. The human mind simply cannot fully grasp the distances involved in outer space.

Even the material of which our earth is made is hard to fully understand. We usually think of such things as rocks, iron, or wood as solid. Actually, all the matter of earth is made up of atoms and electrons in constant motion. There is space between all those electrons. If you squeezed all the atoms and electrons that make up the earth together so they were all touching and had no space between them, the entire earth would become no bigger than the size of a pebble.

Our earth is made up mostly of space. As amazing and mysterious as our material universe is, there is another side to it that is even more mysterious and amazing. It is spirit.

Mind Over Matter

Most serious scientists today will admit there really is something called spirit. We can't study it the way we can study atoms or electrons. We have no instruments to measure spirit. We only know there is some nonmaterial energy that can act on material things. We can see the effect spirit has on matter.

You are spirit and matter, for example. All human beings are. All humans have ability to exert spiritual energy upon their bodies. Some have mastered this ability to an amazing degree.

There are people who can slow their heart rate just by thinking about it. There is one Indian master who can single out and raise just one hair on his head. His mind's control over his physical body is fantastic.

Because spirit does not follow the usual laws of time and space as we know them, some people have demonstrated the power to be aware of things happening thousands of miles away. You have probably heard of cases where some gifted person has helped police in another country find a missing person. He or she can *see* just where the police should look. It is as if this person was right there. The spiritual side of reality and the spiritual side of all of us has become a very popular and exciting field of study today. It is no longer a topic just for ghost stories or religious fanatics.

Because it is popular, some people are trying to make a fast dollar out of it. There are fakes who offer programs and training to misguided people who are emotionally off-balance. These fake programs can do serious harm. We should not believe everything we hear or read. At the same time, being human means being spiritual as well as material. The more we can understand about spirit the better.

Spirit—
Any nonmaterial force or energy that is not bound by the laws of matter, space, or time.

Your Spiritual Nature

Your spiritual nature has been present and at work even before your birth. But it takes some time before you become consciously spiritual and can consciously use your spiritual nature.

Small children, for example, live in a two-dimensional world of things and logic. Time, with its past, present, and future, has a spiritual dimension. Small children cannot understand time except in concrete images. Small children will ask how long it will take to get to grandma's. You say about an hour. They will almost always ask, "How long is that?" It does not do any good to say sixty minutes. You might explain by talking about a favorite TV show that is an hour in length. That they can imagine.

Ideas like truth, beauty, and goodness are spiritual. Small children cannot fully understand what those ideas mean. They can tell something is pretty (beautiful) but they could not tell you what beauty is. They can tell you when someone is good to them, but they could not tell what goodness is.

The capacity to understand the spiritual side of nature and to consciously direct your spiritual powers does not start to operate for most people until their early teens. It continues to develop for some years after it first appears.

Making the Connection

Learning about how the spiritual side of us can affect our material side is interesting. Things like "mind over matter" are fascinating.

Growing in the ability to understand and think on the spiritual level is exciting, too. A whole new world opens up. It's like having new eyes. It's like beginning to see the real world for the first time.

But the most exciting part of becoming conscious of the spiritual in you is the new way you can relate to others. Once you become consciously spiritual, relating to others can take on a new dimension. By seeing things with your new spiritual eyes, you can begin to recognize and appreciate another person's spiritual qualities, something you could not see before.

Parapsychology—
The science that studies the mind's ability to act outside the laws of space, time, and matter.

If what you see in another person is good and beautiful, your own spirit will be attracted to that person. You seek the other person because he or she is good and beautiful. You forget about yourself and any profit you might gain from the relationship. Just being with the other person is enough. Just as important, you find yourself wanting to do good things for the other person. You don't do these things so the other person will do good things for you in return. You do it for the sheer fun of making the other person happy.

A friend is someone who knows your faults but likes you anyway.

That is what love is. That is what true friendship is. Loving is the most powerful spiritual energy you have. Being loved is the most wonderful thing a person can experience. To be fully human, you must be able to love and you must be able to accept another's love for you.

Being fully human is to have spiritual relationships.

False Alarms

Words such as *spiritual, relationship,* and *love* are not your everyday ideas. You will hear them often enough, but they are often misused, watered-down clichés. Love is a good example of word abuse. We hear expressions all the time such as "I just love. . . ." We hear phrases such as "falling in love." We see bumper stickers such as "Lovers have more fun." The worst example of misuse is the expression *making love.*

In the popular sense, the word *love* usually means, "I am physically or emotionally attracted to someone or something because of the pleasure it can give me." The word *love* does not have much weight when it is used over and over. Being attracted to something is okay. Finding another person physically attractive is okay, too. Enjoying a pizza or a rock star's singing is fine. But it is not love.

"God is love, and anyone who lives in love lives in God and God lives in that person." (1 John 4:16)

Why is it not love? Because loving at the spiritual level means forgetting about oneself. It means being happy because the other person is happy. Parents love their children that way.

God loves all of us that way.

Spiritual Bond

What happens when two people love each other on the spiritual level? A bond is formed, a bond so strong poets say it cannot be broken by time, distance, or even death.

Do you belong to any clubs, teams, or activity groups? If you do, you know there is some kind of bond between the members. You all have some common interest, some common goal, or some common task. You work together, you cooperate, you help each other, you follow the rules needed to be sure you can reach your goal. You share the enjoyment of winning the game, putting out a good paper, reaching whatever goal you have. Whatever it is that holds you together, though, is actually outside of you. Once the season is over, the team disbands. Once the school year is over, the club does not meet.

Let's suppose, though, that you became close friends with some person on the team or in the club. You continue to enjoy each other's company long after the season is over or the school year ends. What holds you together is not some common interest outside of you. It is something between you and your friend. You see a goodness in the friend that attracts you. Your friend sees the same in you. You are bound together by this spiritual attraction. That bond could last the rest of your life. You could become separated for years, thousands of miles apart, but if you should meet again that bond could still be there, because the goodness you see in the other is still there. That is love. It's also more.

The reason the spiritual bond of love is so strong is that the two loving persons form a unity. They share the same values. If one is happy, the other is happy. If one is sad, the other becomes sad, too. What makes one happy makes the other happy. What makes one sad makes the other sad. That is what happens when you relate to another on the level of your spirit.

Any Number Can Play

One special thing about the nature of spirit is that it has no parts. It cannot be divided. It is an energy that cannot be used up the way you can use up gas or electricity. That is why you can share yourself with more than one person at the same time. Many people can share in the same friendship together. A whole group of people can become so united that they share the same values, and are eager for the happiness of each other. If one person in the group is sad, the whole group is saddened and seeks to help. If one person in the group has a success or gets some honor, the whole group is happy and feels honored, too. That is what we call community—co-unity. It is like one person, one spirit, in many bodies.

Community—
People who share something in common and who are bound to each other by what they share.

Ideally, that is what families are supposed to be—a whole group of persons bound by a common spiritual bond of loving each other. Where this does exist in a family, you will find a group of very happy people. They might be poor. They might have problems and illnesses. But they are happy. No matter how you look at it, happiness is not rooted in things. Happiness is primarily the experience you have when you are in a loving relationship, in community with other persons. It is sharing your spirit with others. It is the experience of being whole. We humans were designed by God in such a way that we are incomplete if we remain alone, outside of any loving relationship with others. We need others to complete us. Others need us just as much. That is why loneliness is the most unhappy feeling a person can have. One of the cruelest things you can do to anyone—sometimes worse than physical harm—is to put down, reject, or ridicule a person who is trying to become friends or is trying to be accepted into your group. Cliques are killers! If you have any in your school, you know that that's true.

One of the cruelest things you can do is to put down, reject, or ridicule a person who is trying to become friends or trying to be accepted into your group.

That Word Again

We talked in the first chapter about being adult. You can now see that being adult is more than just being responsible and being concerned for others. It is fundamental. It is just common sense. The real core to being adult is to be able to operate out of your spiritual capacities. It means beginning to be able to form spiritual relationships. It means being able to love.

Being adult means more than just having these spiritual capacities. It means using these capacities. You can choose to continue operating at the level of a child, to remain more interested in things than in persons. You can choose to be more interested in yourself and your pleasure than in others and their happiness. Or you can choose to accept the challenge of striving to become more adult.

Being adult means more than just having spiritual capacities; it means using these capacities.

And Then There's God

At the end of the last chapter, we said God wants to be taken seriously. Another way of putting it is that God wants a relationship with us at the level of our own developing spiritual capacities. God seeks to form with us the same kind of spiritual friendship we described above—with a bond stronger than death and with a unity that makes us one with God. God wants a friendship so close that we share the same thoughts, the same values, the same goals.

Once you begin to grasp what God is calling you to, you will begin to realize what it will mean to be confirmed in God's Spirit. But first, we must talk a little more about God's Spirit.

Scripture Search

Read the following passages and be prepared to do these tasks:

1. *Tell the story or main ideas of the passage in your own words.*
2. *Explain how you think the passage relates to the main ideas of this chapter.*
   - *Mark 7:14–23*
   - *Mark 9:14–29*
   - *Mark 10:17–31*

Summary

The spiritual side of reality is far more amazing and powerful than the laws and forces of the material universe. Your own capacity to understand and direct your own spiritual nature is just beginning to emerge. It will continue to grow the rest of your life, if you are willing to work at it. Your greatest spiritual power is the ability to love and to form bonds of friendship with others. Human happiness is rooted in experiencing friendship and community with others. That is how God created us. That is why loneliness or being spiritually isolated from others is the most painful experience we can have as humans. That is also why being spiritually adult means developing and using your spiritual capacity to love others. God wants to be friends with you at this adult level.

Chapter 2: Activities

Activity 1

Below are some activities that show ways in which a person is beginning to operate on the spiritual level. Indicate how often you are doing any of them by circling the word that best says it for you:

1. Concerned about making family members happy

   Seldom Sometimes Often

2. Wondering about your future; making plans for your future

   Seldom Sometimes Often

3. Beginning to wonder what life is all about

   Seldom Sometimes Often

4. Taking time just to think about your life

   Seldom Sometimes Often

5. Helping others just because they need help, not to get some reward

   Seldom Sometimes Often

6. Refusing to do something that gives you pleasure if doing it would make others unhappy

   Seldom Sometimes Often

7. Enjoying the goodness you see in your friend

   Seldom Sometimes Often

Can you think of some people in your class who show most of those qualities?

Do you think they are some of the more mature people in your class?

Do you think they are well-liked by most of the class? Why or why not?

Activity 2

In his first Letter to the Corinthians, Paul tells us the importance of love and then describes what love looks like in action. Read 1 Corinthians 13:1–7, to find out what he says. Think back over the last week. Can you remember some of the things you did that seemed to be acts of loving? List them and what aspect of loving they seemed to show, for example, played a boring game with my little brother—patience and kindness.

Act	Loving Quality
1. ______	
2. ______	
3. ______	
4. ______	
5. ______	

Being able to love and then actually doing loving things is a sign of becoming spiritually mature. How do you think you are doing?

Activity 3

Television programs often talk about love. Many use the word *love* the wrong way. Some try to give you a good picture of what loving means. List some shows you think give a wrong idea about love and some shows you think give a good idea of what love means.

Wrong Idea of Love	Right Idea of Love
1. ____________	1. ____________
2. ____________	2. ____________
3. ____________	3. ____________
4. ____________	4. ____________
5. ____________	5. ____________

Compare your lists with others in the class. Explain the reasons why you rated a show one way or the other.

Would you say that on a typical night there are more shows that give you the wrong idea of love than the right idea?

Activity 4

Read the Scripture passages listed below. Each passage tells something about God's Spirit or what happens when God's Spirit is given to someone. After each passage, write down what you think are some key things it tells you about God's Spirit or what happens when the Spirit works through someone.

1. Isaiah 42:1–3

2. Isaiah 61:1–3

3. Ezekiel 36:24–28

3 Opening Up

The night is clear and balmy. You can smell almond blossoms. A gentle breeze teases the palm trees. Drums, hollowed logs covered by goat skin, throb hypnotically. There are three of them played by three very intent young men. The dancers sway and shuffle rhythmically to the beat. A chant "A-Dah-Dah-Dah-O" rises louder and louder among the dancers and spectators. Bottles of rum are passed around freely.

The drums, the dancing, the chanting continue for several hours without a break. Finally, it happens. Several dancers begin to shout. They babble. They wave their arms wildly. Spectators cheer them on. After a few minutes, they fall into an exhausted swoon and sink to their knees, an indescribable smile on their faces.

The place? A small town on an island in the Caribbean. The occasion? A celebration of *Los Palos del Espiritu Santo*—the Drums of the Holy Spirit.

It is a cult feast that is a strange mixture of Catholic faith and Haitian-based voodoo. The devout attend these celebrations in the belief that they will receive the Holy Spirit and experience the trance described above. Their understanding of the Holy Spirit is somewhat off-base, but no one can fault them for their sincerity.

Now another scene:

The room is plain enough. The people sit on the bare wooden floor. They wear casual clothes. The men and women present range in age from the late teens to the late sixties. There are quite a few Bibles around, on laps, on the floor. There is a sense of peace in the room. Everyone is sitting, eyes closed, praying quietly in murmurs. Suddenly, a young woman of about twenty stands. She begins to speak quickly, loudly, her arms outstretched, her face lifted upward, her eyes closed. But her words make no sense. They are of no known language. One can only sense a feeling of joy, peace, and praise in the tone and expression. The circle of her companions begins to say quietly, almost in whispers, "Praise the Lord" or "Amen" as they listen to this gift of tongues.

The place? A church basement in a town in the Midwest. The occasion? A meeting of a charismatic prayer group in a Catholic parish. Charismatics are a dedicated and growing group within the Church with a very special devotion to and faith in the Holy Spirit.

The Holy Spirit

There is much confusion and wrong information about spirit in general and about God's Spirit in particular. Many stories, movies, and television shows deal with both good and evil spirits. Some people get overly excited when they hear about evil spirits and this adds to the confusion. Some people see spirits everywhere and in everything. Whatever they cannot explain they blame on an evil spirit.

Others go to another extreme. They deny the existence of spirit altogether. They explain spiritual events as hoaxes or as tricks the mind plays on mentally unbalanced people.

The truth lies somewhere in the middle. Much of what people used to consider the work of some spirit can now actually be explained by science. It can be explained by things such as hypnosis, chemical reactions in the brain, or even mental illness. Yet there is a great deal that cannot be explained that easily, and there is strong evidence today of the existence of the spirit world.

We are not interested in those spirits here, though the topic is very interesting. We are concerned about one spirit in particular, God's Spirit. What is God's Spirit like? How and when does the Spirit act in our world and in our lives? Why? How should we try to relate to God's Spirit?

To find the answers to these kinds of questions, we must go directly to the source, to God, and to what God has revealed to us about Himself in the Bible.

Charismatic (care-iz-mat-eek)—
Gifted by the Holy Spirit; devoted to seeking and experiencing special gifts of the Holy Spirit. It is from the Greek word, *charisma,* meaning gift or favor.

Ruah—
The word the Hebrews used for Spirit until almost the time of Jesus.

Ruah

During most of the Old Testament times, people, including the Hebrews, had a rather simple idea about God and spirit. The word the Hebrews used for spirit until almost the time of Jesus was *ruah.* It means breath or wind. Even though you cannot see breath (except on a cold day, of course), you can feel it. The same is true with wind.

Living things breathe. You can feel the breath coming from their nostrils. The wind moves leaves on trees. It can also blow down trees. So ruah came to mean life, the vital force, in living things. It also meant power.

From Abraham's time on, the Hebrew people gradually became convinced that God had no body. God was an invisible, nonmaterial being who controlled all creation and the lives of all people. One of the ways God directed creation was through ruah. The Hebrews did not think God actually breathed the way humans do, but they had no other word to describe the vital force or the power that came from God. Just as they talked of God's breath or ruah they also talked about "His strong right arm" or "the hand of God." They knew God did not have arms and hands or any kind of body, but these expressions helped them talk about God's action and involvement in their lives. God directed, aided, and protected His people with His ruah, His breath, His Spirit.

God's Spirit

Throughout the Old Testament, there is mention of God sending His Spirit upon people. The common expression used in the Bible is "the spirit (*ruah*) of the Lord came upon. . . ."

When God touched a person and shared His power or life force with someone, the results were not always the same. Sometimes it was what you might call a "one-shot deal." For example, in the Book of Judges (chapter 16) we can read how the Spirit of the Lord came upon Samson. It gave him incredible physical strength for the task he faced. He was able to break the strong ropes that his enemies tied him with. Then he was able to kill one thousand armed soldiers using only the jawbone of a donkey as his weapon.

We can find many similar times when God sent His Spirit upon someone to help him or her do a very difficult thing that took special courage or strength. To receive God's Spirit came to mean to receive God's own strength, courage, and power. It also came to mean to receive God's own wisdom or knowledge. Justice and peace were also things people could make happen after receiving God's Spirit.

The word *ghost* is the Anglo-Saxon word for spirit. Until recently the Holy Spirit was traditionally referred to as the Holy Ghost. The Church changed to the word *spirit* because ghost had taken on the popular meaning of a spook in a white sheet.

But the Bible also mentions another way God's Spirit came upon people. Sometimes, it says God's Spirit *rested* upon certain persons. God's Spirit rested upon Moses, for example, and upon David. It rested upon the prophets.

Here the authors were trying to describe how certain persons with special roles to play among the people were aided in an ongoing way by God's power, direction, wisdom, justice, courage, and knowledge. In a sense, their whole lives and all their actions were guided and empowered by the very Spirit of God. They lived by God's Spirit.

One other way the Bible talks about receiving God's Spirit deals with being made holy, being renewed, receiving a whole new way of living. There is the famous story told by the prophet Ezekiel about the dry bones. He describes how spiritually dead, sinful people are raised to a new, holy life when God's Spirit comes upon their dry bones. To receive God's Spirit can also mean to begin to live a totally new way, a holy way, even though you were dead because of being sinful. To receive God's Spirit, for some people, came to mean beginning all over, starting a new, more holy life because God's Spirit now directed their actions.

Next Step

The authors of the New Testament continued to speak of the action of God's Spirit in much the same ways as in the Old Testament. They spoke of the Spirit coming upon someone, of the Spirit resting upon someone, of being reborn in the Spirit, of being filled with the Spirit.

The effect of receiving God's Spirit was described in much the same way, too. It gave people courage for special tasks, it filled them with God's wisdom so they could proclaim the Good News. It gave them peace, joy, and knowledge.

There is one big difference though, when the authors of the New Testament speak about God's Spirit. In the Old Testament, people thought of God's Spirit as an action of God, something apart but flowing from God. After Jesus' death and resurrection, people came to realize that God's Spirit is a Person in the same way as the Father and Jesus. To receive God's Spirit is to come under the direct influence and be in relationship with a Divine Person.

Also, they came to realize that the Father's Spirit and the Spirit by which Jesus lived were one and the same. To be filled with the Spirit of God the Father is to be filled with the Spirit of Jesus.

God Sends the Holy Spirit

All through the Old Testament God kept promising the Hebrews He would one day send a Messiah. *Messiah* means the "Anointed One." The Messiah that God would send would be anointed with God's own Holy Spirit. The role of this Messiah would be to establish God's reign among all humanity. God would do this by sending the Holy Spirit upon us, by sharing God's own Holy Spirit with us.

Red is the color used to symbolize the Holy Spirit. The Church uses red vestments and altar decorations on feasts dedicated to the Holy Spirit.

We know now that Jesus is that Messiah. We also know how He sent the Holy Spirit upon the apostles and other believers at Pentecost. That was the beginning of a new age, the final stage in the history of the world. It happened on the first Pentecost.

When the day of Pentecost came, it found them gathered in one place. Suddenly, from up in the sky there came a noise like a strong, driving wind which was heard all through the house where they were seated. Tongues of fire appeared, which parted and came to rest on each of them. All were filled with the Holy Spirit. They began to express themselves in foreign tongues and make bold proclamation as the Spirit prompted them.

Staying in Jerusalem at the time were devout Jews of every nation under heaven. These heard the sound, and assembled in a large crowd. They were much confused because each one heard these men speaking his own language. The whole occurrence astonished them. They asked in utter amazement, "Are not all of these men who are speaking Galileans? How is it that each of us hears them in his native tongue? We are Parthians, Medes, and Elamites. We live in Mesopotamia, Judea, Cappadocia, Pontus, the province of Asia, Phrygia and Pamphylia, Egypt, and the regions of Libya around Cyrene. There are even visitors from Rome—all Jews, or those who have come over to Judaism; Cretans and Arabs too. Yet each of us hears them speaking in his own tongue about the marvels God has accomplished." They were dumbfounded and could make nothing at all of what happened.

"What does this mean?" they asked one another, while a few remarked with a sneer, "they have had too much new wine!"

Peter stood up with the eleven, raised his voice, and addressed them: "You who are Jews, all of you staying in Jerusalem! Listen to what I have to say. You must realize that these men are not drunk, as you seem to think. It is only nine in the morning! No, it is what Joel the prophet spoke of:

It shall come to pass in the last days, says God,
that I will pour out a portion of my spirit on all mankind:
Your sons and daughters shall prophesy,
your young men shall see visions
and your old men shall dream dreams.
Yes, even on my servants and handmaids
I will pour out a portion of my spirit in those days,
and they shall prophesy." (Acts 2:1–18)

It is now the time in history when God's Kingdom is being established. God's reign over humanity is the work of God's Spirit. The more people allow God's Spirit to *enspirit* them (guide, motivate, and direct them), the more God's reign is established. God rules over the hearts of men and women by sharing His Spirit with them. It is a very gentle, loving way to rule. God's Kingdom is a Kingdom of justice, peace, and fellowship.

Mesiah—
means "anointed one."

Pentecost—
The fiftieth day. Pentecost originally referred to a Jewish feast celebrated on the fiftieth day after Passover to commemorate receiving the covenant at Mount Sinai.

Another Kind of Spirit

The apostle Paul often spoke of the spirit of the world. This spirit opposes God's Spirit and the growth of God's reign. As an example, read Romans 1:18–32.

This spirit of the world is not a person. It is an influence, a force, an attraction that can draw people to do just the opposite of what God's Spirit urges us to do. People can actually be enslaved by this spirit of the world.

It is easy enough to see the effects of the spirit of the world around us. It is the source of greed. It creates oppression of the poor and weak. It causes fights. It causes wars. Whereas the Spirit of God forms us into a loving community, the spirit of the world creates hatred and disorder. It keeps us apart, makes us enemies of each other.

The Holy Spirit teaches us to know the truth. The spirit of the world deceives, lies, and tricks us by promising us all kinds of good things such as wealth and power and popularity. The spirit of the world has been the subject of many movies and television shows over the years. The picture of evil presented in these pictures is one that many people are attracted to. The shows depict people who seek power, wealth, and pleasure. To get it they lie, steal, cheat, and murder. But do you remember how attractive and even likeable those characters seemed to be? Do you remember how fascinating the story was? The spirit of the world is like that. It can make the worst kinds of evil and the most evil kinds of persons seem likeable, attractive, and entertaining. The spirit of the world is, basically, that powerful attraction to evil. All of us experience it to some degree. Fortunately, God's Spirit is more powerful than the spirit of the world.

Satanism—
A cult devoted to the worship of Satan. It is growing today, often attracting curious youth who then become ensnared and controlled by its leaders. Police in most major cities now have special details to keep track of Satanic cults, because they have been known to practice murder and human sacrifice.

Images Help

We just said the Holy Spirit is powerful. That's true. But did you know that one of the most popular symbols for the Holy Spirit is the dove. What is more gentle or less threatening than that pure white, little bird? The Holy Spirit is not a bully who forces us to do what we do not want to do. The Holy Spirit is gentle and peaceful.

In ancient times, olive oil was used as medicine for healing wounds. It gave strength when rubbed into muscles. It was used with perfume in much the same way as we often use cosmetics today. So oil came to be associated with the qualities of health, healing, strength, and beauty.

For that reason, it was often used in important ceremonies. A new king, for example, was often anointed with oil to show that the king would be strong, have good health, and enjoy the benefits of a good reign.

Many times in Scripture, especially in the New Testament, you will read how God anoints us with His Holy Spirit. For that reason, oil and anointing with oil were also associated with the Spirit. To receive the Spirit is to receive the Spirit's healing power and health, to grow strong, to become beautiful in the sight of God. In your own confirmation ceremony, you will be anointed with oil.

Another favorite image of the Holy Spirit is fire, especially tongues of fire, such as the ones that dance on top of a candle or leap up from logs in a fireplace or campfire. Fire is warmth. It is light. It is energy. So is the Spirit of God. The Spirit gives us the warmth of God's love. The Spirit enlightens our minds. The Spirit can fill us with a burning desire to share our God and our God's love with others.

Chrism—
Perfumed oil or ointment. It comes from the Greek word for oil. It is root for Christ—the Anointed One—and for Christian—a follower of Christ.

Some of the common symbols or images the Church uses to help us understand the nature and action of the Holy Spirit include the dove, perfumed oil, fire, and wind.

We already saw how the image of breath or wind was also used to describe God's Spirit. The wind blows where it will. It blows how it will. It cannot be contained or directed. It is free. The Spirit is like that. The Spirit moves among us, it comes and goes at its own pace. We can never force or control the Spirit to do anything. Wind can be gentle. So can God's Spirit. Wind can be powerful. So can God's Spirit. A person is refreshed by a gentle breeze. A person is driven by a powerful gale. God's Spirit can refresh us and can also give us the strength and courage to do things we could never do on our own.

Can you begin to imagine what it would be like if your own spirit and God's Spirit got together? What would happen to you if you formed a personal, spiritual relationship, a friendship with God? What would happen if you allowed God's Spirit to influence you the same way the spirit within your friends already influences you? What would happen to you if you allowed God's Spirit to influence you to the same degree that the spirit of the world influences some people in our society?

We will see that in the next chapter.

Scripture Search

Read the following passages and be prepared to do these tasks:

1. *Tell the story or main ideas of the passage in your own words.*
2. *Explain how you think the passage relates to the main ideas of this chapter.*
   - *Ezekiel 37: 1–14*
   - *Judges 15: 9–14*
   - *1 Samuel 16: 1–13*
   - *Luke 1: 22–32*
   - *John 1: 24–34*

Summary

There is much confusion and misinformation about the meaning of spirit, in general, and the Holy Spirit, in particular. But in Scripture God has revealed to us the correct understanding. In the Hebrew Scriptures, God's Spirit is described as God's "ruah" or breath, the living, life-giving force that comes forth from God to guide, direct, and protect God's people. In the Hebrew Scriptures, God sends the Spirit in several different ways. God's Spirit is given as a "one-time" act to enlighten or empower someone for a special task. God's Spirit is given as a permanent gift; God's Spirit rests upon someone, establishing him or her in a special role, such as a prophet. Finally, through the Spirit, God renews, restores, recreates, or makes holy that which was dead or sinful. In the New Testament, we discover that God's Spirit is a unique Divine Person like the Father and the Son. God's Spirit and the Spirit given by Jesus to his disciples is one and the same Holy Spirit.

The spirit of the world is an evil influence that opposes the Spirit of God and pulls us away from God toward evil. It results in greed, violence, hatred, disunity, disorder, and alienation. Fortunately, the Holy Spirit can overcome the spirit of the world's power over us. Some of the more common symbols or images the Church uses to help us understand the nature and action of the Holy Spirit include the dove, perfumed oil, fire, and wind.

Chapter 3: Activities

Activity 1

Reread St. Paul's Letter to the Romans 1:18–32. Go through one of this week's newspapers. List the headline of each article you feel indicates that the spirit of the world is at work.

1. ______________________________
2. ______________________________
3. ______________________________
4. ______________________________
5. ______________________________
6. ______________________________
7. ______________________________
8. ______________________________
9. ______________________________
10. ______________________________

Now do the same thing, looking for examples of activities where God's Spirit is at work.

1. ______________________________
2. ______________________________
3. ______________________________
4. ______________________________
5. ______________________________
6. ______________________________
7. ______________________________
8. ______________________________
9. ______________________________
10. ______________________________

Activity 2

Scriptures used the dove, fire, wind, and oil as images to describe God's Spirit and how God's Spirit works. Can you think of any other words taken from modern times that might also help us understand the Spirit? One example is electricity—power, light, but invisible.

List as many examples as you can think of, and tell what qualities of God's Spirit each symbolizes.

	Image or Symbol	**Qualities**
1.	______________________	______________________
2.	______________________	______________________
3.	______________________	______________________
4.	______________________	______________________
5.	______________________	______________________

Activity 3

Read the Scripture passages listed below. After each passage, write down what you think are some of the key things it tells you about God's Spirit or what happens when God's Spirit works through someone.

1. Joel 2:28–29

2. Romans 8:14–17

3. Romans 8:26–27

4 From Me to You

If you are familiar with the word *possession* it's likely that you have heard it used in reference to evil spirits. In possession, a spirit takes over another person's body and uses that body in whatever way it chooses. Descriptions of the behavior of people possessed by evil are not very appealing.

There are many accounts in the New Testament about Jesus casting out evil spirits from people. One of the most interesting is the time Jesus came across the "wild man" of Gerasa. It's worth retelling here:

> *They sailed to the country of the Gerasenes, which is opposite Galilee. When he came to land, he was met by a man from the town who was possessed by demons. For a long time, he had not worn any clothes; he did not live in a house, but among the tombstones. On seeing Jesus, he began to shriek; then he fell at his feet and exclaimed at the top of his voice, "Jesus, Son of God Most High, why do you meddle with me? Do not torment me, I beg you." By now, Jesus was ordering the unclean spirit to come out of the man. This spirit had taken hold of him many a time. The man used to be tied with chains and fetters, but he would break his bonds and the demon would drive him into places of solitude. "What is your name?" Jesus demanded. "Legion," he answered, because the demons who had entered him were many. They pleaded with him not to order them back to the abyss. It happened that a large herd of swine was feeding nearby on the hillside, and the demons asked him to permit them to enter the swine. This he granted. The demons then came out of the man and entered the swine, and the herd charged down the bluff into the lake, where they drowned.*
>
> *When the swineherds saw what had happened, they took to their heels and brought the news to the town and country roundabout. The people went out to see for themselves what had happened. Coming on Jesus, they found the man from whom the devils had departed sitting at his feet dressed and in his full senses; this sight terrified them. They were told by witnesses how the possessed man had been cured. Shortly afterward, the entire population of the Gerasene territory asked Jesus to leave their neighborhood, for a great fear had seized them; so he got into the boat and went back across the lake.*
>
> *The man from whom the devils had departed asked to come with him, but he sent him away with the words, "Go back home and recount all that God has done for you." The man went all through the town making public what Jesus had done for him. (Luke 8:26–39)*

Missionaries tell us possession by evil spirits is still rather common in some primitive societies.

It is important to know that evil spirits cannot really do anything that takes away the free will of people. They can use a person's body as a means for speaking, for example. The possessed person can't stop it. But no evil spirit can force a person to agree with what is said or what the body is forced to do under the evil spirit's control.

Another Kind of Possession

Charles Manson, the leader of the group known as Helter Skelter, had a different kind of power over his followers. He and his followers committed a series of brutal murders that people still talk about today. First, he took over the minds of his followers. Then he was able to get them to use their own bodies to do all the killing and robbing that he suggested.

He had a kind of hypnotic power over people. So did Hitler. So did James Jones of the Peoples' Temple. In 1978, Jones was able to convince hundreds of people to commit suicide in Guyana. That's more control than an evil spirit can exercise over unwilling victims. It is a case where people surrendered themselves to the power of another person and his spirit. They allowed themselves to be taken over and they chose to do so. They wanted to do so. This was also the way Manson was able to take complete possession over the lives of his followers.

There is more to it though. Usually, people who can be so sucked in by some cult leader have emotional needs that are not being met. They have some real weaknesses. They are ready to, even want to, give someone else responsibility for what they do and say. They are ripe for brainwashing. That's the kind of possession that certain cults and fanatic movements are rooted in. It is a form of brainwashing innocent, vulnerable people.

Possessed by God's Spirit

God could take possession of your body if He wanted to. Whatever other spirits can do, God can do to a greater extent, because God created everything, including the other spirits. They get their very existence from God.

Clearly, God could take over your mind, too, because God knows all your weaknesses, the things that would make it easiest to control and manipulate you. But God never works that way. God wants and waits for your free cooperation. God does not brainwash anyone. God never takes away a person's free will. You are always able to resist, to refuse to cooperate with God's Spirit when God offers to share it with you.

When you allow God's Spirit to guide and influence you, you become more free, not less free.

To put it another way, you are never actually possessed by God. Instead, God invites you to enter into a union of friendship. If you follow the direction of God's Spirit and are filled with the Spirit's power, it is because you choose to allow it to happen. God wants your love and friendship. God does not need

your bodies or minds as evil spirits and evil persons do. But once you form this friendship with God, you will freely allow God to use your talents and your minds to help Him bring His love and His Kingdom to others. You will do what God wants you to do because you are friends. That is what friendship is all about.

Under the Influence

Let's take a closer look at what happens when you enter into friendship with God and allow God's Spirit to influence you. First of all, you begin to think the way God thinks. You begin to see things from God's point of view. Second, you begin to act the way God acts. That is, you become able to do the things needed to bring about the kind of society of peace and justice God seeks to establish.

We find a summary of what it means to think and act the way God does in what the Church calls the gifts and fruits of the Holy Spirit. They are described in the Bible. The gifts are listed as follows:

- Wisdom
- Understanding
- Knowledge
- Courage (Fortitude)
- Right Judgment (Counsel)
- Reverence (piety or love)
- Awe in God's Presence (Fear of the Lord)

The fruits include:

- Love, joy, and peace,
- Patience and kindness
- Goodness and loyalty
- Gentleness and self-control

Gifts of the Spirit—
Special powers of the Spirit bestowed upon the Church and all its members to enable them to carry out Jesus' mission.

Fruits of the Spirit—
Love, peace, joy, patience, kindness, goodness, faithfulness, humility, and self-control.
(Galatians 5:22–23)

At first glance, these gifts and fruits may not seem so special. You've been told to be kind, patient, and loyal for as long as you can remember. You've been sent to school since you were six so you can learn to know and understand things. Parents and other adults are always talking about the importance of self-control or self-discipline. Who doesn't know that joy and peace are better than gloominess and fighting? So you have a right to ask why these gifts and fruits of the Spirit are so special. We'll try to explain.

Straight from the Source

God is infinite. There are no limits of time or amount when you talk about God. So there are no limits of time or amount when you talk about the effects you experience when you come under the influence of God's Spirit. You share, you participate in the infinite wisdom of God. You experience a kind of peace and joy within you that doesn't depend on what is going on around you. You participate in the unshakable courage, faithfulness, and self-control that God possesses.

Because they are of God, the effects God's Spirit have on you are constant, and they are limitless. They are always there, available for you when you need them. When you allow God's Spirit to influence you, it means God is always right there with you (literally within you!) ready to share with you whatever you may need at the time. Does the situation call for patience? God's patience is available to you! Does the situation call for knowledge or understanding? God is there to share knowledge and understanding with you! Does the situation call for courage? The very courage of God is there to support you!

Are you getting the idea? When you have a good friend, that friend's personality or "spirit" will affect you. You begin to think and act the way your friend does. If you seek God as your friend and companion, if you allow God's Spirit (God's "personality") to influence you, you really do begin to have the capacity to think and act the way God does. Just remember, there are no limits of time or amount to what God shares with you.

Infinite—
To be totally without limits of any kind. Only God is truly infinite.

Gifts and Fruits: What Is the Difference?

Perhaps the best way to describe the difference between the gifts of the Spirit and the fruits of the Spirit is this. Think of the gifts as the special talents or powers or skills of God that God gives to the whole Church. Think of the fruits as the "personal attitudes" you will experience because of your friendship with God.

You don't really receive the gifts as your "personal property." The gifts belong not just to you but to the whole community, the Church, to help the whole Church carry out its mission to promote God's Reign. As a full member of this Church, you share in the Church's mission and, therefore, the gifts will always be available to you when you need them to help the Church carry out its mission.

The fruits, on the other hand, have a certain personal quality to them. They are God-like "attitudes" that help you act God-like in your day-to-day situations. You experience the fruits in a more or less personal way to help you deal with your day-to-day situations in a God-like way. But you experience the gifts (special powers, talents) when you need them to help the Church carry out its mission.

What It All Looks Like in Practice

Jesus described very clearly how people will think and act when they come under the influence of God's Spirit. We find this description—the Beatitudes—in the Sermon on the Mount:

Happy are the poor of spirit;
theirs is the kingdom of God.

Happy are the meek;
they shall inherit the earth.

Happy are those who mourn;
they shall be comforted.

Happy are those who hunger and thirst for justice;
they shall be satisfied.

Happy are the merciful;
they shall have mercy shown to them.

Happy are the pure of heart;
they shall see God.

Happy are the peacemakers;
they shall be called God's children.

Happy are those who are persecuted in the cause of justice;
theirs is the kingdom of God. (Matthew 5:3–10)

To be happy (or blessed) means to be filled with God's Spirit. Those happy people who are filled with God's Spirit will not be enslaved by worldly goods. They will be meek and gentle, rather than bullies. They will experience sadness whenever evil seems to rule society. They will work for justice with their whole being. They will be forgiving and merciful toward the weak and the sinner. They will keep God and God's Reign as their highest priority. They will be peacemakers. Finally, they will be willing and able to endure persecution rather than take the easy way out and give in to evil and injustice.

Beatitudes—
The standards for a happy life given by Jesus in the Sermon on the Mount.

One of the largest, most beautiful churches ever built is the Santa Sophia (Holy Wisdom); it is dedicated to the Holy Spirit. It is in modern Istanbul and is now used as a museum by the Moslems, who captured it from the Christians in the fifteenth century.

That's heavy. To act in those ways means to go against the grain of just about everything today's society holds up as the key to happiness: wealth, power, getting even, looking out for number one, avoiding pain and discomfort at all costs. It should be obvious that no one can think and act like that unless they are filled with God's Spirit. Yet Jesus doesn't hesitate to call His followers to think and act that way. Jesus calls us because he knows that, if we let God's Spirit influence us, we will be able to think and act that way.

Do you begin to get the picture? Through your confirmation, God's Spirit is shared with you in a special way. If you allow God's Spirit to influence you, you will be "happy" (or blessed), and you will be able to think and act in the ways Jesus describes. Are you ready for that challenge?

As Christians, we are the only ones who believe there are three Divine Persons who share one Divine Nature equally. We call this the mystery of the Blessed Trinity. We profess our faith in the Trinity each time we sign ourselves with the Sign of the Cross "In the name of the Father and of the Son and of the Holy Spirit."

If That Is So

You might be thinking that, "If the Holy Spirit does all these things for people when they are confirmed, why aren't there more saints around. I don't see many people walking around showing all that wisdom, joy, fortitude, patience, and other things you call the gifts and fruits of the Spirit."

That's a good point. There is a lot of truth in it, sad to say. The reason is simple though. Keep in mind that God offers people the Spirit and the Spirit's special gifts. People are not forced to accept them or to use them. The Spirit's gifts and fruits are available to us as full members of the Church. We must choose to use them and allow the Spirit to work in us.

The gifts of the Spirit are often represented as seven lamps with seven tongues of fire or as a (mystic) seven-pointed star.

We will talk about that again when we deal more directly with confirmation and what is involved. But be forewarned. Don't expect some miraculous change in you or your companions overnight. Learning to recognize and to take advantage of the Spirit's gifts to you is a lifelong process. You can keep on improving. You have to work at it. First of all, you must want to live by God's Spirit. But what is most important is that these wonderful gifts are available to you. God wants to share the Spirit with you. God wants you as friends. God wants you to be fully alive.

Gifts of the Spirit

Wisdom This is the capacity to see with God's eyes. It is the capacity to see the "big picture" and reduce the most complicated realities to their simplest terms. For example, wisdom enables you to see that all life can be reduced to one simple truth: love of God and neighbor.

Understanding This is the God-like capacity to see beneath the surface of a problem or an issue and to recognize what is really involved. For example, sometimes when people do or say cruel things, they are not actually cruel people. It takes understanding to realize that they may actually be lonely, frightened people who are crying out for help but don't know how.

Knowledge This is the God-like capacity to get the facts straight, to be able to recognize the difference between truth and error.

Courage (Fortitude) Wisdom, understanding, and knowledge enable you to be convinced of what is good, with a God-like conviction. Courage is a God-like strength to be able to hold on to and defend that good no matter how difficult or dangerous it might be.

Right Judgment (Counsel) Gifted by God's wisdom, understanding, and knowledge you will be able to figure out how best to act in a tough situation. You will also be able to help others do the same. To have the gift of right judgment is to always have God's advice available to you when you need it.

Reverence (Piety or Love) Because you are gifted by God's wisdom, understanding, and knowledge, it will be totally clear what it means to be God's beloved child, someone very special to God. This gift enables you to be sensitive to the love and holiness God offers you through Jesus and the Christian community. You'll always want to act the way a grateful and loving child would act.

Awe in God's Presence (Fear of the Lord) Again, gifted by God's wisdom, understanding, and knowledge, you'll have a keen awareness of just how special and awesome God really is. You will know that nothing exists that is more important than God. You will rather cease to exist than deliberately betray God's love for you.

Scripture Search

Read the following passages and be prepared to do these tasks:

1. *Tell the story or main ideas of the passage in your own words.*
2. *Explain how you think the passage relates to the main ideas of this chapter.*
   - *Isaiah 11:1–9*
   - *1 Corinthians 12:1–11*
   - *John 14:10–27*
   - *John 16:4–15*

Summary

The Gospel tells many stories of how Jesus helped people who were possessed by evil spirits. That kind of "being possessed" literally means that an evil spirit resides within a person and controls his or her body to some degree. Though that kind of possession is possible and makes for good horror stories, it isn't that common. There's another kind of "possession" that is more common. It's when strong people (good or evil) exert a powerful influence over their followers and get them to think and act the way they do. Many people became "possessed" in that sense by Hitler, for example.

In somewhat the same way, if we become friends with God we allow God's Spirit to influence us. We begin to think and act in a God-like manner. The kind of influence God's Spirit exerts over us is described in terms of the gifts and fruits of the Spirit that God shares with us. If we become "possessed" by God's Spirit we are truly happy or blessed. We are empowered to think and act in the ways described by Jesus in the Beatitudes taught in the Sermon on the Mount.

Chapter 4: Activities

Activity 1

We all have at some time had a mistaken idea about something which caused us to feel badly or act wrongly until we realized our mistake. For example, when you were little, did you ever worry all day that your parents were going to be very angry when you got home because you got your clothes all dirty playing on the way to school? But when you got home, your parents didn't get angry at all. They took it for granted that little children will play and that little children often get dirty playing.

Give some examples where you had similar kinds of experiences. List the mistaken idea, the feeling or action it caused, and what happened that corrected your idea. An example is provided to get you started.

Mistaken Idea	Feeling or Action	What Corrected It
A certain person was stuck up because he or she avoided you.	You tell everyone that so and so is stuck up.	A friend tells you the person actually likes you but is just shy.

1.

2.

3.

4.

Activity 2

Below are listed the fruits of the Holy Spirit—the feelings and abilities a person experiences when he or she lives by God's Spirit. Rank them in order of the importance each has for you at this time in your life. That is, place a "1" in front of the one you would most like to have, a "2" after the one you would like next and so on until you have ranked them all.

_____ ability to love	_____ ability to be patient	_____ ability to be faithful
_____ have a sense of joy	_____ ability to be kind	_____ ability to be gentle
_____ have a sense of peace	_____ ability to be generous	_____ have self-control

Activity 3

Listed below are the seven gifts of the Spirit. After each one, place the name of some person, living or dead, whom you think displays that particular gift in a special way. Give an example of such an act. (You can use characters from a novel or television shows if you want to.)

1. Wisdom, Understanding, and Knowledge
   Person:

   Example:

2. Reverence (Piety or Love)
   Person:

   Example:

3. Awe in the Lord's Presence (Fear of the Lord)
   Person:

   Example:

4. Right Judgment (Counsel)
   Person:

   Example:

5. Courage (Fortitude)
   Person:

   Example:

Activity 4

Read the Scripture passages listed below. After each passage, write what you think are the key things it tells about God's Spirit or what happens when the Spirit works through someone.

1. Galatians 5:22–25

2. Ephesians 4:1–6

3. Ephesians 4:13–19

5 Born Again

A few years ago, there was a teenage gang leader in Brooklyn named Nicky Cruz. He was about the toughest guy in town. He and his gang were into everything. They had rumbles, or fights, with neighboring gangs where people actually got killed. They played for keeps. They mugged, and they staged holdups and burglaries. They used drugs and they used girls.

The law of averages says Nicky should be in jail today—if he hasn't already been killed in some fight. Do you know what he's actually doing? He goes around the country speaking at youth rallies telling the young people about Jesus and about giving themselves to Jesus.

There was a minister named David Wilkerson who started working in Nicky's neighborhood. He started telling Nicky about Jesus. At first, Nicky resisted. He was afraid of nothing, but for some reason he was afraid of that "skinny preacher," as he called Rev. Wilkerson. He even threatened to kill him. But Wilkerson kept going to Nicky. In time, Nicky had a deep religious experience. He came to believe in Jesus.

That's when he left his life in the streets and ended up preaching about Jesus. This kind of complete change of life—from sin to faith in Jesus—is often called a rebirth. People who have the experience call themselves "born-again Christians." It's as if they really are born all over and begin to live a totally different life.

The Church and Being Born Again

Being born again is often considered a very personal experience, as an individual thing—"between me and God." The Catholic Church looks at it differently. The Church started out as a group of people, followers of Jesus, who were reborn as a group. Their rebirth was a community experience. It was the rebirth of a community.

Centuries ago God established a community through Abraham. God also led them out of slavery in Egypt through Moses and made them into the Jewish nation. Some remained faithful to their community religious identity. Some did not. Jesus, the Messiah promised by God, called the faithful ones to a new and deeper identity and the unfaithful ones to repentance. Many did not listen. Among those who listened were the apostles, who may have spent as much as three years with Jesus. They lived with him, ate with him, worked with him, and learned from him.

Together they shared the terrible pain and disappointment of Jesus' crucifixion, though most of them abandoned him at his most difficult moment. Together they also shared the wonderful experience of his resurrection when he was with them once more. Through their common experience of following Jesus, going through his crucifixion, and finally seeing him again in his risen state, they came to realize Jesus was, in fact, the Messiah God had promised to send to the children of Abraham. This discovery of Jesus as the Messiah was a shared experience. His resurrection sealed their common faith in Jesus as God's Chosen One.

A short time after his resurrection, Jesus left this little community of believers. But they did what Jesus had instructed them to do. They went back to Jerusalem, gathered together in a large house and waited. They prayed while they waited. Then it happened. Jesus sent his Spirit upon them. The Spirit was given to the total group, not just to individuals. The Spirit rested upon the community and came to dwell there. Christians believe that they identified themselves as the Old Testament family of Abraham experiencing a rebirth on that day. They became the New Testament family. A community was reborn. The Church was born!

And there is more to it than that. It is true that when the Holy Spirit rested upon that little band, God's Spirit "confirmed" them in their rebirth, in their faith, and in their union with Jesus. At the same time, the Spirit enlightened them, empowered them with the gifts of the Spirit and then sent (the Gospel word is "drove") them forth with the mission to tell all who would listen to this Good News of God's Salvation. They were sent forth to invite all people to a similar conversion and rebirth. You see, one of the main tasks of the Church, having been reborn itself, is to continue throughout all of time and in all the world the work Jesus began on the shores of Galilee: the establishment of God's Reign among us. At Pentecost, the Church was not simply born; it was also empowered, equipped, and sent forth into the world to proclaim God's Reign and to call all others to a rebirth similar to their own.

Conversion—
To change from one religion or set of beliefs to another. But, more fundamentally, it means to turn one's whole self around to God, to change one's heart and be "reborn," to try to grow spiritually. In this sense, we are all called to ongoing conversion as disciples of Jesus.

Joining the Community Means Being Born Again

When the apostles, newly alive with the Spirit of Jesus, began to tell the Good News that Jesus was the long-awaited Messiah, many of the Jewish people listened—and believed. They wanted to become members of this reborn community of Abraham's children.

Stop and think a minute. What were the key experiences that led to the apostles' own rebirth?

Jesus' death and resurrection—especially the resurrection—was one. The other was receiving the Spirit on Pentecost. It was very natural that these two key events ought to be experienced in some way by the new converts in order to become members of the reborn community.

But how? Guided by the Spirit, the apostles chose two kinds of actions the people were familiar with: baptism and the laying on of hands.

Baptisms were already a common practice for the Jewish people. There were washings or baths that had a religious meaning. Baptism signified ritual purification, initiation into the Jewish faith, or washing away sins. The apostles added a new meaning, or symbolism, to baptism, though. Going under the water was like dying and being buried, just as Jesus died and was buried. Coming back out of the water was like coming back to life, just as Jesus was raised from the dead by his Father. Death to sin and the former self, birth to forgiveness and life in Christ.

Paschal Mystery—
The term used to describe God's plan and action to rescue humanity from sin and death and restore us to fullness of life and holiness in Jesus. Christ's passover from death to life through His saving passion, death, and resurrection.

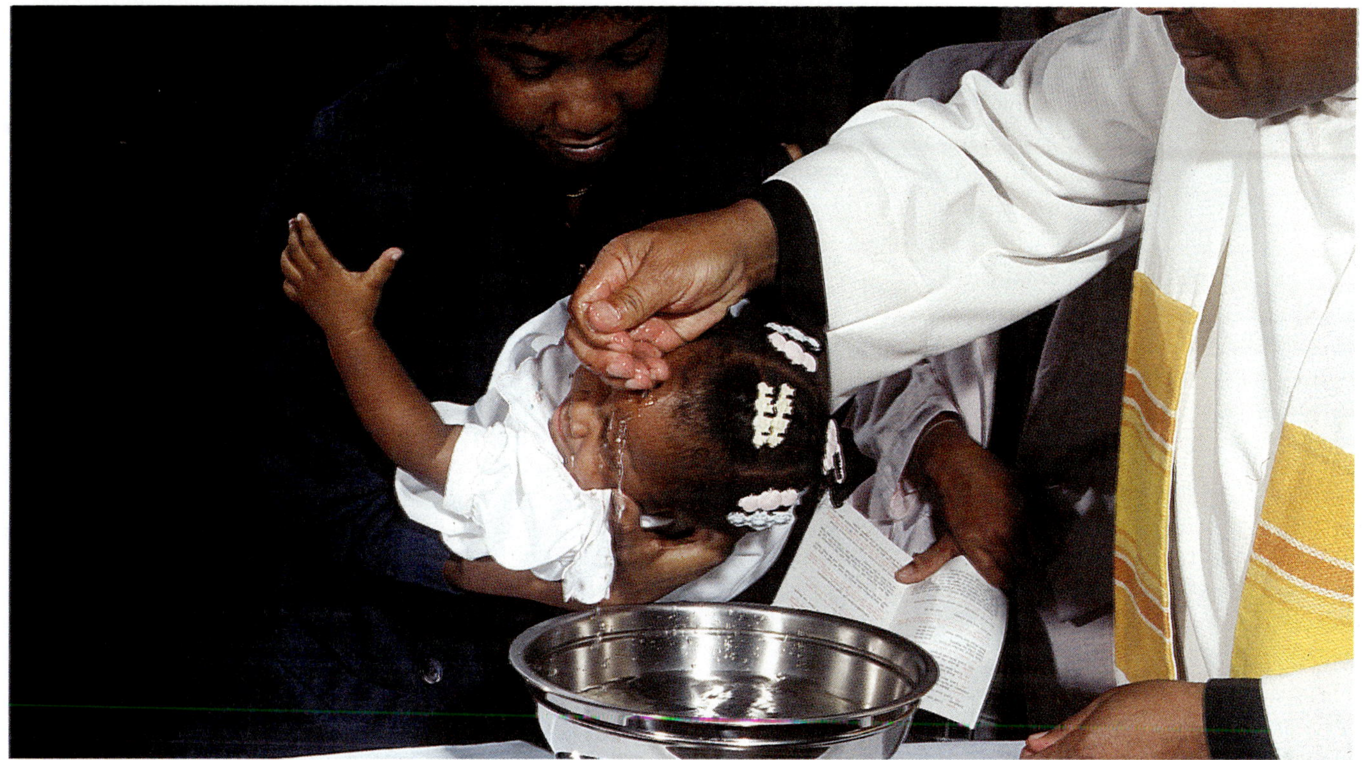

The Paschal Mystery is partially revealed in the Hebrew Scriptures through the events of the Passover, Exodus, and Covenant. In the New Testament, it is fully revealed in the events of Good Friday, Easter Sunday, and Pentecost.

By baptism, the new convert could go through, in a symbolic way, what the apostles had experienced firsthand. When Jesus died, all of the mistaken hopes and dreams of the apostles died, too. When Jesus reappeared, the apostles began to live again. But more than that happened to the apostles. It was not until they received the Spirit at Pentecost that they came to realize that they didn't just come back to life. Life after Pentecost had a totally different meaning. They were fully alive with and lived by the Spirit of Jesus. Their rebirth was completed.

So, besides baptizing the new converts, they also "laid hands upon them." This gesture was a common practice at that time. Parents would lay hands on their children as a way of blessing them. It was a sign that the power and life of the parents would pass through the parents (through their hands) and come to rest upon the children.

That's why, after the baptism, the apostles would lay their hands upon the heads of people coming out of the water. It was the apostles' way of sharing the power of the Spirit they themselves had received on Pentecost.

Once a person was baptized and confirmed, he or she was considered a full member of the reborn community of Abraham. They were members of the new people of God, the Church.

Getting Organized

The Church started with maybe 120 members on the first Pentecost. Becoming a new member was simple then. A baptism and the laying on of hands was all that was necessary. As time went on, the community grew rapidly. It needed to become better organized. It also had time to think about all that Jesus said and did—aided now by Jesus' own Spirit who dwelt in the community.

That's why the Church began to include the Eucharist as part of the initiation ceremony. After baptism and confirmation, the new converts were allowed to join in the Eucharistic banquet where they could receive the Body and Blood of Jesus for the first time. This was the final sign that they were full members of the reborn community where Jesus and his Spirit dwelled. Baptism-Confirmation-Eucharist became the three-in-one rite of initiation.

In addition, other signs and symbols were added to the process of being initiated into the reborn community. Candles, especially the paschal candle, began to play a key part. The new converts needed sponsors. Converts were expected to reject their pagan name and take a new name, as a sign of their rebirth. In the ceremony, the new members put on white robes as a sign of their new, pure life. Formal prayers developed. The ancient practice of anointing was added to the laying on of hands.

Because many new converts were pagans who knew very little about the history of the Old Testament and what the very idea of Messiah meant, they needed a longer period of instruction than a speech like the one Peter gave on the first Pentecost.

A formal period of instruction began. It developed into the season we now call Lent, the period before Easter. As a result, Easter became the official time for bringing new members into the reborn community. The ceremony began on the Easter Vigil, the night before Easter. It ended with the celebration of the Eucharist just after midnight.

Pagan—
Term used to describe anyone who does not believe in God as revealed in the Scriptures—a heathen, an irreligious person.

Lent—
The forty-day period of prayer and fasting before Easter. It begins on Ash Wednesday. The season when we prepare to celebrate the mystery of Jesus' death and resurrection and deepen the conversion symbolized and begun in our baptism. The time of final preparation for new converts before they are initiated into the Church at the Easter Vigil.

In our Eucharist, we recall, celebrate, and reexperience the Paschal Mystery of Jesus' death and resurrection.

Times Change

Obviously, some things have changed. You were probably baptized into the Church as an infant. You participated in your first Eucharist at about age seven, when you were in second grade. Now you are preparing for confirmation.

Don't worry. There is nothing wrong with such an initiation by stages. There are many reasons why the initiation rite got split up like that. It's a long, complicated story so we won't get into it here. The real problem is that by separating the baptism-confirmation-Eucharist ceremony, confirmation tended to get lost in the shuffle. Its real nature and meaning became blurred.

For one thing, baptism, which is always received as the first of all the sacraments, began to be considered *the* sacrament of initiation. That was the "biggie" in terms of assuring persons that they were included in Jesus' saving death and resurrection. Eucharist came to be seen as the special sacrament it is in terms of receiving Jesus' body and blood. Its role as part of initiation into the community was lost.

The seven Sacraments are grouped and described in various ways. One way is:
Sacraments of Initiation: **Baptism, Confirmation, and Eucharist.**
Sacraments of Reconciliation and Healing: **Reconciliation, and Anointing of the Sick.**
Sacraments of Vocation: **Matrimony, and Holy Orders.**

If baptism guaranteed that you could now be counted as a member of the Church, and gave you the special privilege of the membership, namely Eucharist, what was left for the Sacrament of Confirmation? In a sense, nothing. Yet, because of the tradition of the early Church, people still considered it important. After all, it was a sacrament.

But the sacrament of what? That's when ideas like "becoming a soldier of Christ" or becoming a "mature Christian" came on the scene. It got so bad that many people never bothered to be confirmed. It was considered an extra sacrament, a bonus. It became the kind of thing only certain people did.

Sacraments—
Sacred effective signs (rites using special words, gestures, and symbols) instituted by Jesus and enacted by the Church through which we experience the saving, healing, and empowering presence and action of Jesus. There are seven sacraments in the Church.

You and Confirmation: What Really Happens?

Through the signs and symbols of your baptism, you experience the death and resurrection of Jesus, much like the apostles did. By this baptism, you become identified with Jesus and with the community where he continues to be present in a special way.

But, like the apostles, your rebirth is not really complete until you finally experience Pentecost. Confirmation is your formal Pentecost. Through Pentecost, the Spirit who has already been given to the community fully becomes your Spirit, too. Your formal Pentecost makes you a full member of the Church. As a full member, you have access to the gifts and fruits the Spirit gave to the Church on Pentecost. Your rebirth is completed. You begin to live in this new life of the Spirit.

Confirmation—
A sacrament through which those who have been baptized in Christ share more fully in the gifts of the Holy Spirit and in membership in Christ's Church.

The feast day celebrated fifty days after Jesus' resurrection to remember the outpouring of the Holy Spirit upon Jesus' first followers is called Pentecost.

Even though your Pentecost experience isn't likely to be as dramatic as the first Pentecost, it is just as real. The first Pentecost was so exciting because a whole community was being reborn. It was one of the major events in the history of the human race. All the special signs that surrounded the first Pentecost helped people see just what was happening. They were necessary then. That community, the Church, has been around for two thousand years now. There is no longer any need of all the external fireworks each time new members share in the Pentecost experience at their confirmation.

Your confirmation is the occasion for a parish celebration. There will be joy and excitement. But whatever feelings, emotions, and external celebrating there are at your confirmation is not as important as the fact that you become a full member of the Church on that day.

It is through being a full member of the Church that you will begin to discover Jesus and his Spirit who are present in the community. It is an ongoing thing rather than a once and for all experience. Each year, Jesus and his Spirit become more visible to you, more important. More and more you will find yourself living by Jesus' Spirit. You will grow into it.

But there is more. Your Pentecost also empowers and equips you to begin to share the Church's responsibility to go out and proclaim God's Reign. Your confirmation literally commissions you to go forth to tell others, by word and deeds, of the Good News of God's love for us. Your confirmation sends you forth to invite others to a similar conversion and rebirth. Your confirmation commissions you as a witness, an "apostle." (*Apostle* means "witness," by the way.)

Confirmation Means Commitment

Through confirmation, the Church accepts you as a full member in the Church. The initiation started at your baptism is completed.

You are expected to take your membership seriously. The Church asks you to make a commitment. Commitment means to give oneself completely to something.

You are being asked to give yourself to active membership in the Church. The reason is simple. It is especially within the community and its shared life that you will discover Jesus and his Spirit. If you stay on the fringes of that community, nothing happens. If you spend little time working, praying, and celebrating with that community, you will have very few opportunities to experience Jesus and his Spirit.

Your confirmation is not some kind of magic that automatically changes you. Your confirmation gives you full membership in the Church.

But for anything to begin to happen, you must use this membership and take on the responsibilities that go with it. It's the same as belonging to the YMCA or YWCA organization. Membership gives you the right to use the pool, gym, and other things. But if you never go and use them, your membership isn't doing a thing for you. Having your name on a membership card won't keep you in shape or give you a fun time. You have to do that yourself. Membership in any organization means opportunity only.

The same is true of your membership in the Church. It's not enough to have your name on the register as a confirmed member. You must try to act like one. It takes commitment.

In the next chapter, we will see what that means in more detail.

Outside the Church

We have been saying that Jesus and his Spirit are present in the community we call the Church. The Church and its members are often called the Body of Christ and the Temple of the Holy Spirit. That's how completely Jesus and his Spirit are present in the Church. But this does not mean people can discover Jesus or receive his Spirit only by joining the Church. It simply means we can be certain that Jesus and his Spirit are available to us as members of the Church. It is Jesus' special guarantee. We can be sure of it.

So if others come to know Jesus and receive his Spirit in other ways, without being members of the Church, we can all be happy for them. But we should also be happy and grateful that we have been called by God to be members of that community where we are certain we can find Jesus and receive his Spirit. That call and our faith are very special gifts indeed.

Scripture Search

Read the following passages and be prepared to do these tasks:

1. *Tell the story or main ideas of the passage in your own words.*
2. *Explain how you think the passage relates to the main ideas of this chapter.*
   - *Exodus 6:2–9*
   - *Psalm 105*
   - *Acts 8:26–40*
   - *Acts 9:1–19*

Summary

At the heart of faith is the experience of conversion, of turning one's whole self to God, of being "reborn." There is an individual quality to conversion, but the Church began with a conversion or "rebirth" of a whole community of people, the apostles and the first disciples of Jesus. This community then began to call others to accept the salvation God offers through Jesus. Those who accepted turned from their past life. They were reborn as new members of this community, the Church. The apostles and first disciples experienced a dying and rebirth through their firsthand experience of the events of Good Friday, Easter, and Pentecost. The new converts experienced their rebirth and initiation into the Church in a sacramental way through baptism and confirmation, followed by Eucharist. As the Church grew, it developed a long period of preparation and instruction for the new converts ending with the initiation rites at the Easter Vigil. Over time, however, confirmation became separated from baptism as the other half of this conversion/initiation process.

Your own confirmation completes your initiation as a full member of this reborn community. You will have the rights of a full member. Your confirmation also gives you the responsibilities of a full member. It empowers and commissions you to begin to take part in the Church's mission to share this Good News with others, just as the apostles began to do at their own confirmation. So, if you are willing to seek confirmation, it means you are also willing to take your faith seriously. It means you are willing to share the responsibility of the Church to promote God's Reign of peace and justice.

Chapter 5: Activities

Activity 1

The apostles used symbolic actions and objects as a means of sharing with converts their own experience of Jesus and of Pentecost. Think of some special group you belong to—your family, this class, some team or club.

A. Now try to identify any experiences this group has had that had a special meaning (for example, your class won the school spirit award, or your club went to Disneyland last year as a reward for a service project).

B. Suppose someone else now wants to join this group. In what symbolic way could you share with them something of the experiences that have a special place in your group's history?

C. Develop a short initiation rite with some words and gestures you would use:

1. Words:

2. Gestures:

3. Symbols:

Activity 2

In the first column, list all the things you are proud to have achieved or mastered that have demanded some real commitment from you.

In the second column, list all the things you are now trying to achieve or master that are demanding a real commitment from you.

In the third column, list all the things you are proud to have that did not demand any real commitment on your part. Examples of each are given.

	Already Achieved	**Working at It**	**No Effort Required**
	honor roll	learning guitar	sense of humor
1.	______________	______________	______________
2.	______________	______________	______________
3.	______________	______________	______________
4.	______________	______________	______________
5.	______________	______________	______________

Activity 3

Below are a list of some of the ways the Church has been described or symbolized. Rank them in the order that best describes for you what the Church is all about. One—best, two—second best, and so on.

____ Body of Christ

____ Temple of the Holy Spirit

____ New People of God

____ Pilgrim People

____ Mother

____ Prophetic Community

____ Christ's Flock

____ Family of God

Using your first choice, list the kinds of things that word or image tells us about the nature of the Church.

Compare your choices with those of others in class.

Activity 4

Read the Scripture passages listed below. Write down what you think are the key things each passage tells us about God's Spirit or about what happens to a person who receives God's Spirit.

Acts 19:1–6

Matthew 12:28–32

Mark 1:9–11

6 Stand Up and Be Counted

When young men and women finish medical training and begin practice as doctors, they know their study and training are not over. They continue to learn and to grow in the skills of their profession all their lives. Or at least they should. When rookies make a professional team and sign the contract, they know their work is just beginning. It takes more than making the team to become a successful professional athlete. It takes ongoing dedication to practice and training. Even teachers who have taught for twenty years continue to go back to school in the summer to sharpen their skills and keep up with new developments in their field. Famous rock musicians practice as much as eight to ten hours a day to prepare for a concert. This is after they have already become famous.

The same thing is true about being a full member of the Church. You should see your initiation at confirmation as the beginning rather than the end of your efforts to become a full member of the Church and a truly adult Christian.

As you continue to grow, there are three things you will want to work at developing: your skills at membership, your capacities for being in touch, and your willingness to go public. We will explain each of these in this chapter.

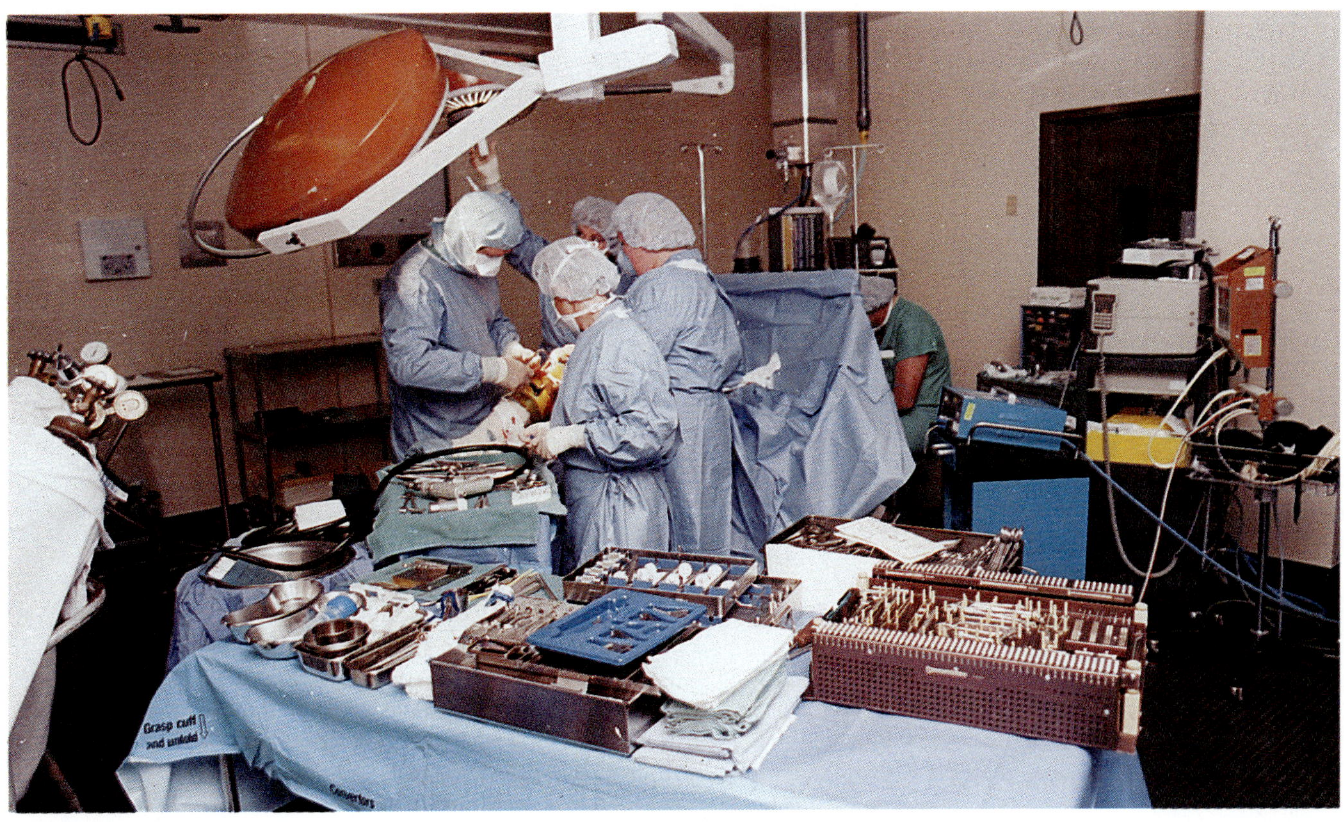

Being a Good member

Throughout the last chapter, we stressed that confirmation is not a private or individual thing provided only for your personal benefit. Any benefit you gain personally by being confirmed into full membership in the Church depends on the degree you participate in the life of the Church. Membership itself is a privilege. It is through becoming an active member that you discover Jesus and his Spirit in the midst of the community.

It is by working and celebrating with the community that you most fully experience Jesus, and come to experience the gifts and fruits of the Spirit, who dwells in the community.

Too often, young people will complain that they feel nothing has really changed for them after confirmation. But if they make no effort to act like full members, nothing can happen. A full member gets involved, cooperates in what the community is attempting to do, contributes his or her time and talents, offers suggestions for how the community might improve or solve its problems. It is by getting involved in the life of the community that you discover Jesus working there among its members. Then a lot happens!

A good example of nonparticipation is the Sunday Eucharist. You will hear many people both young and old complain that "I don't get anything out of it." Their experience is a common one. So is their mistake. They forget that the Sunday Eucharist is a community celebration. It is not something put on for an individual "to get something out of." It is a community celebration of thanks for all that God has done for us. It offers us the opportunity for a community experience, not a private one. If we do not participate with the other members in the celebration there is no way to get anything out of it. It would be like going to a party and refusing to join in the dancing and games. The more each person joins in at a party—or at the Eucharist celebration—the more the whole group grows closer together and goes away happy.

A good member, then, becomes involved, active in the life of the community. He or she participates and contributes. If the community has a problem—and all parishes have some problems—the good member does not just sit around and complain. He or she seeks a solution and offers to help. Is the singing poor at the liturgy? Offer to join the choir or help form one. Is parking a problem on Sunday mornings? Offer to help direct parking or paint lines in the parking lot. Does the parish lack good social programs for the youth? Get some friends together and come up with a plan you can suggest to the parish council. You have every right as a full member of the Church to take that kind of action. In fact, you have a responsibility to do so. And, if you use your new found adult capacities in the process, you will be taken seriously.

A good member, then, is one who is involved in the community's life more than forty or fifty minutes on Sunday mornings. He or she takes the time to find out just what organizations, groups, and programs the parish sponsors and then offers his or her talents where they are needed.

Catechumenate (kata-kew-men-ate):
The official process for preparing new converts for their initiation into the Church. A convert enrolled in the process is call a *catechumen.*

Communion of Saints:
The community of both the living members of the Church and all those faithful members of the Church who have lived before us.

Koinonia (coin-oh-nee-ah):
The Greek word for community.

If being a member means getting involved, it also means education. Good members know the community to which they belong. They know its history, its heroes and heroines, the great things it has done in the past, the great things it is trying to do in the present. The more you know about the tradition of this community we call the Church—what it believes and what it has done—the prouder you will be to have been accepted as a full member. You belong to the community of such giants as St. Francis of Assisi and St. Teresa of Avila. It is important for good members to know the history of their local parish community, its past heroes and its present leaders. It's all a part of belonging.

Being in Touch

Prayer is a very important part of your growth as an adult Christian and full member of the Church. Over and over, we say that Jesus and his Spirit are present in the community of which you are becoming a full member. It is possible to be a very active member in that community and still not see Jesus and his Spirit. The skill needed here is developing as a prayer (pray-er).

Being a pray-er means you are working at becoming more and more in touch with Jesus and his Spirit in your day-to-day life.

Being a prayer is a little different than saying prayers. It is more a basic attitude and a way of looking at things. Pray-ers fully believe that Jesus and his Spirit are present in the community and in their own everyday life. For that reason, prayers are always on the alert to recognize the signs of that presence and to discover what it is Jesus and the Spirit might be saying to them.

To do this, they take time as often as possible, certainly a little time each day, to think about what they are experiencing. Journal keeping has become one popular way for doing this. There are many others. One of the oldest is reading Scriptures and asking what the Scriptures might be saying to them about their lives right now.

Some people prefer to do this kind of thing in small groups. As this skill for recognizing Jesus and his Spirit develops, prayers discover that Jesus and his Spirit can communicate with them through just about any person or event that touches their lives. A friend's correction, a parent's praise, the Sunday homily, the sudden death of a classmate, being elected chairperson of some committee—Jesus and his Spirit can communicate with us through just about anything. The trick is learning to recognize Jesus and his Spirit when they do.

What do they communicate? Whatever is important for us at the time. Maybe you're down on yourself, really beginning to feel like a loser. Some friend drops by and cheers you up, gives you some much needed encouragement. You begin to feel better about yourself. Jesus could very possibly be working in and through your friend's kindness. Or some friend may warn you that you are making a lot of people angry by your "know-it-all attitude." Jesus could be present to you then, too.

You could be working through a really tough personal decision. Something the priest says in the Sunday homily hits you right between the eyes. You suddenly know what you should do. Is Jesus speaking to you?

Becoming a prayer, then, is the skill you will need to stay in touch with Jesus and his Spirit. It means reflecting, taking time, talking with God about your life. It's what a good member of the Church works at every day. The reason for staying in touch should be obvious. The more you become aware of what Jesus and his Spirit are saying to you, the more you can shape your life and your decisions around Jesus and his Spirit. Isn't that what being a full member of the Church is all about in the first place?

The expression most often used in the documents of Vatican II to describe the Church is "People of God."

There are many road blocks to becoming a prayer today. Most of us live at a very fast pace. It is hard to find the time to be quiet and to reflect. That's why you must take the time rather than find it. In addition, our lives are filled with a lot of clutter. Radios blaring, television sets going, instant news about every strange thing that takes place in the world today from mass murders to some crazy new cure for cancer. We usually have to dig through all this clutter to get at what is important that is happening in our lives.

We have to work at being prayers. But any effort we make will be worth it.

Going Public

Today the word *witness* usually has a very legal meaning. Persons in court are called to tell what they know or saw in regard to some crime. They give testimony.

In the early Church, the idea of being a witness was quite different. The first members of the Church felt they had one basic mission in life: to tell everyone what they knew about Jesus and what they saw him do. They were to give testimony about Jesus to whomever would listen, wherever they would listen. It wasn't a legal idea then. It was "shouting the good news" about Jesus and the Kingdom of God. It was their mission. But they gave their message, their testimony, by more than words. Their whole lives as individuals, and more importantly as a community, were visible testimony about the reality of Jesus and God's Kingdom.

When the Holy Spirit comes upon you, you will be filled with power and you will be witnesses for me, even to the ends of the earth. (Acts 1:8)

You probably know that the word *martyr* means someone who is killed for believing in a cause; someone who willingly sacrifices his or her life for a cause. Did you know the original meaning for *martyr* is "witness," someone willing to give testimony? The early martyrs of the Church willingly sacrificed their lives as a means of "bearing witness" or testifying to the truth about Jesus and God's Kingdom.

Witness—
To share the good news of Jesus Christ in word and in actions.

Martyr—
One who sacrifices his or her life for a cause.

The idea of witness, of being a witness, of having the mission to tell the world about Jesus is still very much alive in the Church. Even physical martyrdom—giving testimony by willingly dying for Jesus—is very much alive. There are martyrs in many parts of the world today, for example, in some countries in Latin America. Even in our country, there are political martyrs, such as, Martin Luther King, Jr.

From the first Pentecost, when the Church was born in the Spirit, the community felt a need to go public. Peter bravely went before the crowd and started "telling it like it is." Full membership in the Church means being a witness—and if necessary a martyr-witness—as much today as it did on the first Pentecost.

Getting Practical

Being confirmed means being sent forth to be a witness. You are being asked to help people come to know Jesus and the values Jesus taught. You are being asked to help people discover that God loves and cares for us and seeks our happiness. (That's what God's Reign is really all about.) All that can sound like a tall order for someone your age. What does it really mean for someone your age to be a witness?

Remember the Beatitudes we listed back in chapter four? Any time you respond as a "Beatitude Person" in a day-to-day situation you are helping people discover what Jesus stands for and what the Reign of God looks like. For instance, take the statement, "Blessed are the meek." Can you walk away from a fight? If someone puts you down, calls you a name, or embarrasses you, can you resist the impulse to return the favor? If you and your parents have a disagreement, can you talk it through without turning it into a shouting match? Are you a gracious loser? Can you congratulate the other person or team and really mean it?

According to a recent study, this is how youth relate to helping others (the poor, the sick, the elderly, those unable to help themselves):
10%—have helped others more than five times a year.
37%—have helped others one to four times a year.
53%—have never become involved.
To which group do you belong?

Are you getting the idea? If meekness really becomes a part of who you are, then you'll be showing people about Jesus and about God's Reign every time you respond with meekness instead of with the force or violence so common in today's society.

Let's take another Beatitude: "Blessed are those who hunger for justice." Can you come to the defense of someone who is being unfairly teased or who is the target of cruel gossip that can destroy his or her reputation? Are you willing to avoid cheating on tests even though everyone else seems to be cheating? Are you willing to go public and join some group or program that is trying to fight drug use and teen drinking? How do you deal with racial prejudice if it is present in your school and neighborhood? Do you try to challenge the racial slurs and comments? Most of these are everyday opportunities you have to challenge injustice and to witness to the Good News of God's Reign.

It's the same for all the Beatitudes. If you are poor of heart, you will often find yourself sharing your goods, your time, your self with someone who might need you. You'll find yourself being merciful, able to forgive and forget, when it would be easier and more satisfying to "get even." You'll find yourself trying to be a peacemaker, trying to help enemies become friends. In short, anytime you live the Gospel, you are giving witness to the Gospel.

If you have been trying to live the Gospel, if you've been trying to be a "Beatitude person" (even when you didn't realize that is what you were doing), then you know firsthand that "persecution" is one of the Beatitudes. For lots of reasons, many people fear and resist the peacemakers, the meek, the merciful, those who seek justice. Because of this fear, they often persecute such "Beatitude people" by ridiculing them, by trying to make them look foolish, by ignoring them and keeping them out of the "in" group. If you've experienced some of this at times, it is a sure proof that you have been giving witness to the Gospel, even if you didn't know what it meant.

Virtues are habitual actions that promote the good of the individual or of society.
Theological Virtues: faith, hope, and charity
Moral or Cardinal Virtues: prudence, justice, temperance and fortitude.

Not to Worry

If you are catching the drift of what we are saying, it shouldn't surprise you if you are also thinking "I'm not ready for all this. I've got enough to worry about just taking care of myself. Besides, I'm nowhere near being that kind of 'Beatitude person' you're asking me to be."

If those are some of your thoughts, don't worry. First, keep in mind that when you are sent forth to witness as a result of your confirmation, you aren't being sent out alone. The Spirit comes upon you (literally resides within you). The Spirit remains with you to enlighten and empower you with His Gifts. When an opportunity to give witness happens, when a Beatitude response is called for, the Spirit will be there to help you see what to do and to empower you to do it.

Second, no one is expecting you to become an instant success, or to act as if you've become a saint. Your mission to be a witness is a lifelong mission. You have a lifetime to grow into being a "Beatitude person." Your confirmation doesn't make you an instant saint. It does get you started. That's all. You're going to fail, often. You're going to miss opportunities to act the way a "Beatitude person" acts. Sometimes, you'll know what you should do, but you'll be too afraid to do it. That's to be expected.

Do you see the relationship between the theological and moral virtues and the gifts and fruits of the Holy Spirit?

The main thing is to keep trying. Remember, because of your confirmation you are called and sent out to help others discover what Jesus and God's Reign is all about. You are sent to do this in your family, in your school, in your neighborhood, in the situations of your day-to-day life. If you keep trying, even if it is only a little at a time, you'll grow into the task. You'll become a "Beatitude person."

Member, Prayer, Witness

You are being challenged to be an involved, participating member; to be a prayer; to be a witness. Full membership in the Church means all three.

Confirmation is not an empty ritual. It is not on the level of a graduation ceremony. It is a rebirth. You are about to be reborn. If you accept the challenge, if you are willing to be reborn, if you accept your rookie status, congratulations. You can count on the veterans to both welcome you and help you meet the challenges that are ahead. They also want to count on you to help them do the same.

Scripture Search

Read the following passages and be prepared to do these tasks:

1. *Tell the story or main ideas of the passage in your own words.*
2. *Explain how you think the passage relates to the main ideas of this chapter.*
   - *Matthew 5: 1–12*
   - *Matthew 6: 5–15*
   - *Acts 2: 42–47*
   - *Acts 7*

Summary

As a result of your confirmation, you are being asked to become an involved member of the community, a prayer, and a witness. It is by being involved in the community that you experience the real effects of your confirmation. It is by working and celebrating with the community that you most fully experience Jesus, and come to experience the gifts and fruits of the Spirit, who dwells in the community. Being a pray-er, basically, means that you are working at becoming more and more in touch with Jesus and his Spirit in your day-to-day life. Finally, being a witness means helping others discover Jesus and experience what God's Reign is really all about. You give witness to this Gospel (this Good News) by doing Gospel things. Basically, that means striving to become a "Beatitude person." But be patient. Becoming a good witness is a lifelong task. The Spirit remains with you to help you.

Chapter 6: Activities

Activity 1

How well do you know your parish community? See if you can fill out this questionnaire.

1. Name of Parish ____________________
2. Address ____________________ Rectory phone __________
3. Pastor's name ____________________
4. Associate pastor's name(s) ____________________
5. Date parish was founded ____________________
6. Name of first pastor ____________________
7. Number of families in parish now ____________________
8. Does your parish have a parish council? ____________________

   Name of president of parish council ____________________
9. List all the parish organizations you know about

   a. ____________________ f. ____________________

   b. ____________________ g. ____________________

   c. ____________________ h. ____________________

   d. ____________________ i. ____________________

   e. ____________________ j. ____________________
10. How many students are in the parish school? ____________________

    Name of principal ____________________
11. How many students in the Parish CCD program? ____________________

    Name of Director of Religious Education ____________________
12. What is the parish's debt? ____________________
13. What percent of the total parish members are over sixty-five? ____________________
14. What percent of total parish membership do not attend Mass or contribute to the Church? __________
15. Does the parish celebrate its feast day? ____________________

Activity 2

As a means of helping you grow as a prayer and of helping you take the time to work at it, fill out the following based on what you are really going to try to do:

1. Best time for me to pray and reflect on weekdays ________________
2. Best time for me to pray and reflect on weekends ________________
3. Best place for me to pray and reflect ________________
4. Amount of time I plan to spend________________
5. Method I plan to use (describe briefly):

6. Biggest problem I expect to face in trying to do all of the above:

7. Possible means I have to overcome this problem:

Activity 3

Once in a while you will hear of someone who takes a group of hostages—as in a prison riot—and refuses to release them until the news media gives the world his or her special message. They may want the whole world to know about the conditions in the prison. It is a means of getting the message across.

Let's imagine you have an opportunity to give the whole world a message via world-wide television. You are allowed to say twenty-five words. You choose this as an opportunity to give witness to your faith in Jesus. Write down what you would say:

Activity 4

Read the Scripture passages listed below. Then write down what you think are the key things it tells you about God's Spirit or what happens when people live by the Spirit.

Matthew 5:1–12

Luke 10:21–24

Acts 1:3–8

7 A Brand New Ministry

A few years ago, a young soccer team and some members of their families were flying on a chartered plane from Montevideo, Uruguay to Santiago, Chile for a game. They lost their course in a storm and crashed high in the Andes. Of the forty on board, thirty-two survived the crash itself, though many were seriously injured. They had no food, water, or clothing suitable for survival on the snow-covered mountain peak, where temperatures dipped below zero each night. As a result, many died.

Yet more than sixteen are alive today. They had survived over ten weeks on the mountain before they were finally rescued. Why? Because they kept hope. And because they worked as a community, each person giving what talents they had. A few were medical students. They aided the injured and became the community's "doctors." Some were physically stronger than the others. They went on scouting expeditions and were able to bring back needed supplies on occasion. Some even managed to eventually reach civilization and bring back the rescue teams.

Others were able to keep up the group's spirits with their humor, their talent for music, and their religious faith. Leaders emerged. A few came up with ingenious ideas for making warm clothes and making shelter from the plane's remains. Everyone contributed. Everyone rose to the occasion.

Another Time, Another Community

The history of the Church's survival is just as amazing. It started with about 120 people, all followers of someone executed as a criminal. They were hated by the leaders of their own nation. They were opposed by Rome, the most powerful government in the world at the time. They had no money, no political clout or military force, no allies or friends. Yet, within three hundred short years, their religion became the official religion of the western civilized world and numbered in the millions.

The secret of their success? It was not their own talents but the special gifts the Spirit gave to each member of the community formed on Pentecost. St. Paul describes it this way:

> *There are different gifts but the same Spirit; there are different ministries but the same Lord; there are different works but the same God who accomplishes all of them in everyone. To each person, the manifestation of the Spirit is given for the common good. To one the Spirit gives wisdom in discourse; to another the power to express knowledge. Through the Spirit one receives faith; by the same Spirit another is given the gift of healing and still another miraculous powers. Prophesy is given to one; to another power to distinguish one spirit from another. One receives the gift of tongues, another, that of interpreting the tongues. But it is one and the same Spirit who produces all these gifts, distributing them to each as he wills.*
>
> *The body is one and has many members, but all the members, many though they are, are one body; and so it is with Christ. It was in one Spirit that all of us, whether Jew or Greek, slave or free, were baptized into one body. All of us have been given to drink of the one Spirit. (1 Corinthians 12:4–13)*

In chapter four, we described the gifts and fruits enjoyed by those who are united to Jesus' Spirit. The gifts are what you might consider common property. They are available to all members of the Church because they were given to the entire community on Pentecost.

That's why we have been making such a big deal about confirmation as initiation into this community. The gifts and fruits become your property, too, to the degree that you fully identify with the community and work at being in touch.

The gifts Paul talks about in this letter are not quite the same. They are not given directly to all members of the Church. They are given to individuals to be used for the Church and to help all the members. Not everyone is given the gift of teaching, for example, but everyone can benefit when the person with the gift uses it well.

Paul is telling us, then, that every person who becomes a full member of the Church receives some special gifts, some special ways in which he or she can serve the other members and help the Church do its work. That means you, too.

Gifts Are for Unwrapping

Being a good member of the Church means participating. That is just common sense. It is what everyone is expected to do.

In a family, for example, all the members can make their own beds. It takes no special talent to take out garbage, wash dishes, or cut the grass once you reach a certain age. Somebody has to do it and if it is your turn—or your job—you do not expect special praise or thanks for doing it.

But in most families, each person also has some special talents to contribute to the common good of the family. Someone may have a special knack for fixing things. Someone else may have a gift for listening or for making others laugh. Someone else may have musical talent. These are unique contributions to the family. But if the gifted people refuse to share their gifts, everyone loses.

That's what we are talking about when we talk about ministry in the Church. Ministries are special gifts. The official word is *charisms*, the Greek word for gifts.

You share a common ministry with all members of the Church because of your confirmation. You are expected to be a witness, to give good example, to help others discover Jesus through you and the way you live.

You also receive special gifts and a special call to minister within the community. It comes from the Spirit. It is the result of uniting yourself to Jesus. The Spirit wants to enrich the Church by enriching you. You, in turn, are enriched by the gifts the Spirit gives to the other members of the community.

Minister—
Comes from the Latin for little or less. In the spirit of the Gospel, a minister is supposed to be a servant to others.

Paul Is a Good Example

Paul started out as Saul, a devout Jew who felt responsible for stomping out the upstart Christian sect that was corrupting the Jewish people. He was good at what he did and took it seriously. He pursued Christians like a bloodhound and threw them in jail.

After his conversion and his initiation into the Church, he still had all his natural enthusiasm. But now he lived by Jesus' Spirit. The Spirit gifted him with the ability to preach to the Gentiles, using his natural ability for a new purpose. He was so successful in winning new converts to the Church, that he ranks with Peter in helping develop the Church born on Pentecost. That's pretty good for a person who started out trying to destroy the infant Church.

***Catechesis* (kata-kee-sis) comes from a Greek word meaning "to echo." A catechist is also called a religion teacher today. The task of the catechist is to "echo" the truth Jesus taught and to nurture others' faith in Jesus and that truth.**

The Spirit enriched the Church by first enriching Paul. Paul enriched the Church by first entrusting himself and his natural talents to Jesus and his Spirit through becoming a member of the Church.

You definitely have natural talents. You are in the process of entrusting yourself to Jesus and his Spirit through your confirmation in the Church. You will be enriched by the Spirit because of it. You will be expected to enrich the Church as a result.

Only 46 percent of youth feel they have good communications with their parents.

Finding Your Gifts

You have been given a great deal to think about. You are expected to be adult. Then you are expected to make a commitment to the community where Jesus and his Spirit dwell. Not only that, you are expected to get excited about it, and put in your time, talents, and money for that community. And you have special gifts from the Spirit you are expected to share with the community. Don't worry, you can handle it.

First, the Spirit builds on what you already have received from God by birth. You will never be asked to do anything you are not capable of doing. Second, you grow into your special gifts over a period of time. Paul did not start out a great preacher to the Gentiles. He had some natural talents and some natural enthusiasm. But it took him some time to discover and to be successful at what turned out to be his charism—apostle to the Gentiles.

You may not know for some time yet what your special gifts and your special role in the Church will be. Just remember that you have one. How do you find out what your special gifts are? You find out by experimenting.

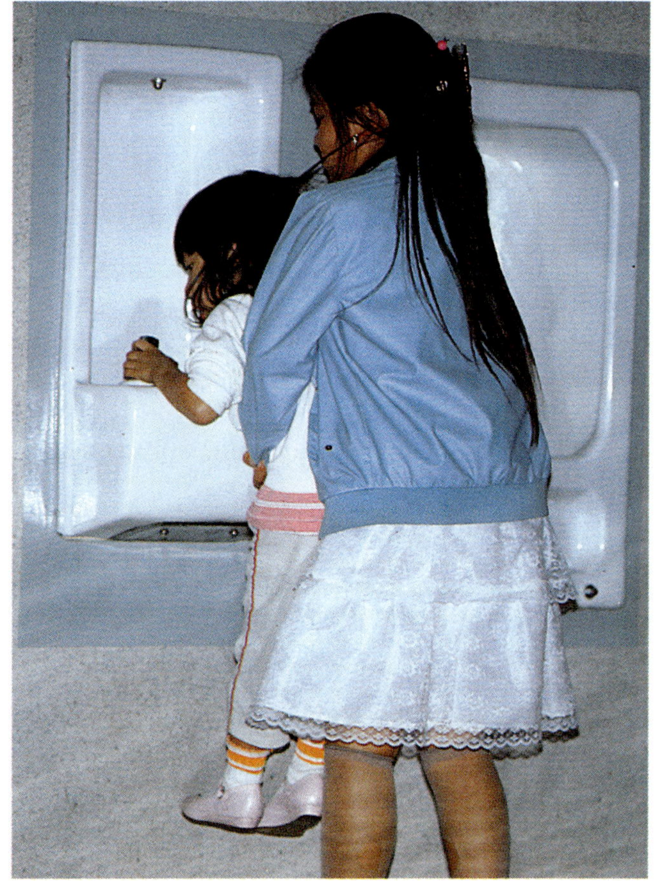

The ministry of a prophet is to speak out. By speaking out, the prophet tries to help people recognize the action of the Holy Spirit in their lives. The prophet also helps people recognize and turn from the influence of the spirit of the world.

Ministry with a Capital "M"

The Church has been assigned certain official tasks or ministries to carry out. These have their roots in what Jesus himself did during his lifetime. Jesus was a prophet and teacher; Jesus was high priest; Jesus was a shepherd/servant. So there are three main kinds of official ministries in the Church:

Ministry of the Word This includes evangelization, catechesis (religious education), theology, and preaching.

Ministry of Worship This includes ordained priesthood and all those ministries related to worship and the celebration of the Sacraments: lectors, musicians, ministers of the altar, ushers, Eucharistic ministers, and so forth.

Pastoral Ministry This includes leadership and administration of the community, one of the main ministries of the bishop. It also includes ministries of caring for those in need of spiritual and physical guidance, help, or healing.

When someone is called and officially assigned to do one of these ministries in the name of the whole community, we might call that person a minister with a capital M, so to speak. To become a Minister with a capital M, you obviously need to have some gift or charism for that ministry. For example, you couldn't expect to be made a Music Minister if you have no talent for music. Besides the natural charism for a ministry, it usually takes some special training to become a Minister with a capital M. Even if you have a gift for teaching, you can't be expected to be assigned to direct the parish religious education program (be the Catechetical Minister) if you have had no special training in what and how to teach.

An evangelist is a messenger sent to tell people the Good News of God's salvation in Jesus and about the coming of God's Reign. Evangelization is a primary ministry of the Church.

So being a Minister with a capital M is a kind of official position in the community. You probably won't be ready to become a Minister with a capital M right after your confirmation. You'll need time to discover what gifts or charisms you may have. Then if you want to become a Minister with a capital M, you'll have to seek special training.

Deacon—
Comes from the Greek word, *diakonia*, meaning "service." A deacon is a servant. You can read how the Church first called forth deacons in Acts 6:1–7.

Prophet—
Comes from the Greek word meaning "to speak out."

Evangelization—
Comes from the Greek word *evangel*, meaning "messenger, an announcer of good news."

Pastoral Ministry—
Comes form the Latin word for shepherd. A person engaged in pastoral ministry cares for, guides, heals, and protects the members of the Church in the name of Jesus, the Good Shepherd. (Read John 21:15–17.)

Unofficial Ministry

You don't have to become a Minister with a capital M to become involved in ministry. As part of your preparation for confirmation, you are being asked to do just that: to become involved in ministry. It is often called a service commitment. You promise to help out in some way within the parish or in your local community.

Remember, this service commitment is over and above what can be expected of you simply because you are a member of the community. As in your family, your parish has chores that need doing. It's only fair that you take your turn when it comes to doing parish chores, like cleaning up after a picnic or pancake breakfast.

Your service commitment, on the other hand, should involve doing some form of ministry in an unofficial way. You don't have to become the Music Minister to volunteer to sing in the choir. You don't have to be Catechetical Minister to volunteer to babysit the children of the parents who are teaching. You don't have to be the Pastoral Minister to volunteer to help an elderly person in your parish do his or her shopping, or give up some Saturdays to help collect food for the poor, or to help take mentally handicapped children to the zoo or the circus.

A Common Mistake

One of the hardest lessons to learn when you begin to serve within the Church is how to deal with failure and lack of gratitude. In one parish, a group of eighth-grade students organized a food drive. After they collected the food, they distributed it to a number of poor families just before Thanksgiving. When they gathered afterwards, they all complained about the fact that very few of the families seemed grateful or said thanks for their gifts and hard work.

St. Paul was a tentmaker by trade and continued in that work in order to support himself while he carried out his ministry. It is possible to mix a profession with ministry.

They did not realize how painfully embarrassing it is in our society to be poor and to have to depend on others for the very food you eat. By not acting overly grateful, poor people can manage to hold on to some shred of self-respect. Being overly grateful is too much like groveling when you are poor. These youth also did not realize that service is its own reward. One does it because one can, and because it needs to be done. Knowing that some poor people will have a decent meal on Thanksgiving is the real reward. Praise and gratitude are nice. Accept them anytime they are available. We all need a pat on the back once in a while to keep us going. But do not fall into the trap of doing service just for the praise or just to get people to think you are nice.

Success is another kind of trap. Sometimes people in ministry, especially if they are getting started, think they should be successful all the time—and right away. They forget that ministry is often a cooperative effort and that it is ongoing. St. Paul described it like this: "One sows, another waters, but God gives the increase." For example, you might try very hard to get your friend to stop fooling around with drugs. She does not seem to listen to you, but at least you have planted a seed. Sometime later, maybe after a bad trip, she remembers your advice and kicks the habit.

You had a part in her conversion even though you might never realize it. Much of the service you will give to the Church is like that. You do not always see the results of your good work right away. You will become very discouraged and stop trying at all if you forget that.

It Works Both Ways

Perhaps, one of the best things about ministry or service is that you come off a receiver in the very process of giving your own gifts.

A group of high school ninth-graders "adopted" a nursing home as a service project. Each week, they would visit the elderly, read to them, chat with them, write letters for them, or play games, such as checkers. In first planning the project, they all expected it would be very difficult and boring, but they knew it would be good for the elderly. What they soon discovered is that they, not just the elderly, were being enriched.

They were amazed at the cheerfulness of the elderly. They were fascinated by all the stories of the "good old days" that the elderly loved to share. They got a warm glow because the elderly were so appreciative of their visits. Most of the time, ministry is like that. You discover that the very people you seek to serve have very much to give to you in return. People who work with the retarded always say that. You'd think the retarded would have nothing to give, but that is not the case. If you try helping them, you will soon find out.

In other words, never fall into the trap of assuming a "you need me—I do not need you" attitude toward the people you serve. Expect, look for, and be grateful for all that the people you serve have to offer you in return.

Not a One-Shot Deal

Sometimes people think that the service projects associated with a confirmation program are a one-shot deal. It is seen as a requirement, a kind of test you go through as part of qualifying for confirmation. Once you finish your project or put in the agreed-upon time, it's over.

In fact, as a confirmed member in the Church, you are committed to a lifetime of service. It may take different forms at different times in your life. But as you discover your special charisms or gifts of ministry, you are expected to share them with the community in an ongoing way. Service is a way of life for a confirmed Christian. Ministry is what the Church is all about.

So any service projects related to your confirmation should be seen as a warm up, a kind of gradual introduction into a life of ministry. Each year, after your confirmation, should see you becoming more involved in ministry. The Church really does need you and the special gifts you will receive from the Spirit. You are being called to enrich the Church. Please take that call seriously.

Any Time, Any Place

There is a passage in Matthew's Gospel in which Jesus describes what He expects of His disciples by way of pastoral ministry or service to others. He calls His disciples to feed the hungry, to cloth and shelter the poor, to welcome the stranger, to care for the sick, to visit those who are imprisoned. (Read Matthew 25:31–40.) This passage is what the Corporal Works of Mercy are based on. The Corporal Works of Mercy are human actions, motivated by love of God and neighbor, relating to the bodily needs of others. The Spiritual Works of Mercy are seven charitable works encouraged by the Church related to the spiritual well-being of others.

The Corporal Works of Mercy are:

- Feed the hungry
- Give drink to the thirsty
- Clothe the naked
- Visit the imprisoned
- Shelter the homeless
- Visit the sick
- Bury the dead

In a real sense, this is the ministry to which your confirmation calls you for the rest of your life. You don't have to ever become a Minister with a capital M. You don't have to make some kind of formal service commitment. As a disciple of Jesus, you are called to a life of ministering to those in need. You can do it any place, any time.

How, you ask? Maybe there are very few poor people in your area who lack food or clothing. You aren't allowed to visit prisons. Perhaps, you don't know any sick people or strangers. But is there anyone in your class—or in your own family—starving for a word of encouragement? hungering for a pat on the back, a little praise, a little recognition? When was the last time, for example, you told your mom or dad what a great job they do in caring and providing for you?

The Spiritual Works of Mercy are:

- Convert sinners
- Instruct the ignorant
- Counsel the doubtful
- Comfort the sorrowful
- Bear wrongs patiently
- Forgive all injuries
- Pray for the living and the dead

There are probably people in your school imprisoned by loneliness, fear, shyness, awkwardness. Couldn't you "visit" someone simply by asking him or her to join you for lunch in the cafeteria, or by saying "hello" each morning? Some may be imprisoned by physical or emotional handicaps. Can you reach out to them? What about the kid everyone thinks is "strange." What could you do to make that person feel welcome. What could you do to help that person become accepted by others? That's welcoming the stranger. Also, someone can feel "naked" when fully clothed, if he or she can't afford the expensive sneakers or jeans or whatever happens to be "in" right now. Can you help such a person feel accepted?

Do you get the idea? Sure there is Ministry with a capital M. There is organized if unofficial ministry you are asked to do as a service commitment. But in the long run, the ministry you are called to by your confirmation can be done any place, any time simply by being attentive to the day-to-day hurts and hungers and needs of the people around you at school and in your own family.

Scripture Search

Read the following passages and be prepared to do these tasks:

1. *Tell the story or main ideas of the passage in your own words.*
2. *Explain how you think the passage relates to the main ideas of this chapter.*
   - *Matthew 5:38–6:4*
   - *Matthew 25:31–46*
   - *James 2:14–17*
   - *Acts 6:1–7*

Summary

Everyone who is baptized and confirmed is called to ministry. Ministry in the Church is not quite the same as the everyday "housekeeping chores" of the parish. The ministry best suited for you will be based on your natural talents and gifts. You discover these gifts by experience and by trying different kinds of service. There are two levels to ministry. There is what could be called ministers with a capital M. Ministers with a capital M are persons assigned to do certain official tasks of the Church in the name of the Church. Such ministers usually need specialized training. Even if you are not a Minister with a capital M, you are still called to become involved in ministry in an unofficial way. You can do this kind of unofficial ministry any time, any place simply by reaching out to help others in your family, in your school, in your parish, in your neighborhood. Don't expect people to always be grateful when you attempt to minister to them. Do expect that you will often receive more than you are able to give when you try to minister to others. Your confirmation service commitment is intended as a warm up for a lifetime of ministry.

Chapter 7: Activities

Activity 1

This chapter points out that there is a difference between housekeeping chores in the parish and ministry within the parish. Give examples of parish housekeeping chores you could do that take no special gift but are the responsibility of all. In the second column, list as many forms of ministry as you can think of within the parish that do require some special gifts from God. An example of each is given.

Parish Housekeeping Chores	**Ministries**
1. helping at the Church picnic	leadership
2.	
3.	
4.	
5.	
6.	
7.	
8.	
9.	
10.	

Activity 2

List two (more if you can) talents you know you have that could be used by your parish. Then identify all the possible groups, organizations, or activities within the parish where these talents could be put to use.

Talent	**Possible Parish Uses**
1.	1.
2.	2.

Now list some possible service commitments you could make as a means of practicing the art of ministering.

Activity 3

Listed are the Corporal and Spiritual Works of Mercy. After each one, identify one concrete act you could do within your own parish that would be a form of carrying out that service.

Corporal Works of Mercy

1. Feed the hungry ____________________
2. Give drink to the thirsty ____________________
3. Clothe the naked ____________________
4. Visit the imprisoned ____________________
5. Shelter the homeless ____________________
6. Visit the sick ____________________
7. Bury the dead ____________________

Spiritual Works of Mercy

1. Convert sinners ____________________
2. Instruct the ignorant ____________________
3. Counsel the doubtful ____________________
4. Comfort the sorrowful ____________________
5. Bear wrongs patiently ____________________
6. Forgive all injuries ____________________
7. Pray for the living and the dead ____________________

Activity 4

Using 1 Corinthians 12:4–13, identify the special gifts God has given to the Church through the Spirit. Can you give an example of any of those gifts you have actually seen being used within your parish?

	Gift	Example
1.	______________________	______________________
2.	______________________	______________________
3.	______________________	______________________
4.	______________________	______________________
5.	______________________	______________________

8 My Confirmation

In some high schools, it is still a custom for seniors to initiate the incoming ninth or tenth graders. The initiation is often rather cruel, a kind of exercise in humiliation. The new students might be expected to sing the school song on demand, wear beanies, or give up their place in the cafeteria line to the older students. You probably know some of the things the new students must do.

In many schools, though, the custom has been changed to something much more sensible. Each new student is assigned an older student as his or her sponsor. The sponsor tries to help, not harass, the new student. The sponsor will explain the school's rules, help figure out the schedule, give tips about the various teachers and school organizations. In general, they try to make the new student feel welcome. It's a kind of Big-Sister, Big-Brother program.

In the early Church, there was something like that. Converts were given a sponsor, or sometimes several, to help them get ready for initiation into the Church. The sponsors would explain the Scriptures and the teaching of Jesus to the new converts. They would help them get involved in the life of the Church and introduce them to the members of the community. The sponsors would also keep an eye out for any bad habits or moral weaknesses that might need to be corrected and would help the converts work at this. They would help the converts begin to develop a prayer life. The sponsor's task was an important one.

Through the Ages

Most converts in the early Church were adults. Many had no relatives who were already Christians. Sponsors seldom were related to the new convert.

In time, the custom of baptizing infants took over in much of the Church. The parents of the infant were naturally the ones most responsible for seeing that the infant was instructed in the faith as he or she grew. They were the natural sponsors. But the idea of having other sponsors was kept alive. It took the form of godparents. The parents would select a couple, usually relatives of the infant or very close friends of the parents. Except for the baptism ceremony, these godparents played little part. They did not have a real role in the education of the growing child.

Things got a little more confused once baptism and confirmation came to be celebrated at different times. The persons to be confirmed were expected to choose a sponsor again. You would think the sponsors should be the godparents of baptism, since confirmation is a conclusion to the same initiation rite begun at baptism. But often others were chosen. Also the role of the sponsor was lost. Because the persons to be confirmed already belonged to the Church from infancy, sponsors had little to do in terms of what the sponsors of the early Church did.

Sponsors and You

Earlier, you were asked to choose a sponsor for your own confirmation. The Church has certain standards a person has to meet before he or she can serve as your sponsor. As you found out, the standards are just common sense. First, your sponsor has to be baptized, be confirmed, and have received the Eucharist. Second, your sponsor has to be at least sixteen years old. (The Church may make exceptions to this rule in very special cases.) Third, your sponsor needs to be a person of faith, that is, a practicing Catholic.

Sponsor—
A person who undertakes the responsibility to guide a confirmation candidate in the preparation for receiving the sacrament. It is the sponsor's role to present the candidate to the Church at the time of the celebration of the sacrament.

The Church encourages you, if at all possible, to choose as your sponsor the person who served in that role when you were baptized. Because baptism and confirmation are two parts of the same initiation, this makes sense. But the confirmation sponsor does not have to be your baptismal sponsor.

You are not allowed to choose your parents as sponsors, but they can certainly take part in helping you in the many ways in which the sponsor is supposed to help you during this preparation time. Also your parents can represent at confirmation a sponsor who cannot be present for some reason.

What are you really looking for in a sponsor? Your sponsor should be a person you consider a mature and dedicated member of the Church. He or she should be a person who can truly help you in many ways. The sponsor should be able to help you understand the teaching of Jesus and help you live out that teaching. A sponsor should be able to guide you and help you become familiar with your parish's activities. A sponsor should not be afraid to point out bad habits and help you work at overcoming them. Therefore, the choice of a sponsor should be taken seriously. You should seek a person who not only can help you become a better Catholic, but also has the time to help you prepare for confirmation.

New Name

In the early Church, many adult converts had received names at their birth that came from pagan religions. One of the signs of their total rejection of that former life and their rebirth into the life of Jesus was to drop the old name and take a new one. The new name was selected for its meaning to the Christian community. Names like Fidelia (faithful) or Theophilus (love of God) or Christopher (Christbearer) were chosen. As time went on, people often selected the names of saints of an earlier time—such as, Peter, Mary, or Paul. Choice of name was taken seriously. One's name was intended to express the quality of one's person and the ideals a person would strive to develop. To choose the name Paul was a kind of pledge to try to imitate Paul's courage and dedication in spreading the Gospel, for example. Mary or variations of Mary were popular for obvious reasons. Jesus changed Simon's name to Peter (rock) because he wanted Peter to become as firm as a rock and a solid base for establishing the community.

At confirmation, you will be asked to give the name by which the bishop will call you. The Church strongly suggests that you use the Christian name you received at baptism. This tends to show the unity between baptism and its completion in confirmation.

But you are also free to choose a second name at this time which becomes your confirmation name. In either case, the name you use at confirmation should be important to you. It should have special meaning, and it should express something of what you hope to become as an adult Christian.

Some young people are tempted to choose a name at confirmation because it "sounds nice." But if you choose a name other than your baptismal name, it should not be based on how it sounds. It should be based on what the name means to you. Think it over carefully. Ask advice from your sponsor. Your new name should mean a new start for you. Your new name should be a challenge for you to grow.

Shepherds used the staff (crosier) to drive off animals threatening the sheep. They used the hook on the end to rescue sheep that had fallen into holes or crevices. The crosier symbolizes the bishop's shepherding responsibility to protect and care for the faithful in his charge.

When the Day Comes

In the early Church, we saw that confirmation was celebrated as part of a threefold rite: baptism, confirmation, and first Eucharist. Today, the Church reunites these three rites in your confirmation ceremony.

The ceremony includes a renewal of your baptismal vows as a kind of reliving of your baptism. Then there is your confirmation. Finally, the Eucharist is celebrated and you join in the banquet with the community. So your confirmation is actually like the full initiation ceremony of the early Church. Let's take a closer look at what will happen and what it all means.

The Celebrant

In the early Church, when the number of members was small, there was usually only one Christian community or parish in a town. Even if there were several communities in the larger towns, there was still only one person who was considered the leader of the communities. For example, Peter was the leader of all the Christian communities in Rome. The leader, or bishop, was the one who celebrated the initiation of new converts into the total community.

As the Church grew, and baptism and confirmation became separated, things changed. A bishop was often the leader of many communities in many cities in an area or diocese. The priest, the leader of the local community, would celebrate the baptisms of the infants as they were born. But each year or so, the bishop would visit the local communities and celebrate the confirmation of those who were ready.

That's pretty much how it is even today. In confirmation, the important thing to remember is that you are being confirmed as a full member in a Church that is a diocese, a community that is much larger than just your local parish.

In addition, the celebrant at your confirmation is an official representative of that worldwide Church community. He is welcoming you into a worldwide community.

Diocese—
An area or district of the Church, which a bishop governs. The bishop is ultimately responsible for the guidance of all the parishes and all the Catholics in his diocese. The word comes from two Greek words meaning "to keep house" or "to govern a house."

Miter—
The tall hat worn by the bishop at official ceremonies. It is a symbol of the bishop's responsibility to serve as a leader in the Church, as the first apostles did.

Crosier—
The staff carried by a bishop. It is modeled after the shepherd's staff with a hook at one end.

Things Familiar

Whether your confirmation takes place within a Eucharistic Celebration or not, the first part of the rite is still, basically, the same as at Mass. There will be a procession of the celebrant and his assistants. You, your sponsors, and sometimes your parents, may be part of the procession, too. You may sit in a special place up front. It's your day. There will be music and singing. You might be asked to help choose the songs. There will be a greeting. Then there will be three readings from Scripture. If you are being confirmed on a Sunday or other major feast day, the reading will be those assigned for that Sunday or feast. But if the readings assigned for the day are not used, the first reading will usually be chosen from the following Old Testament passages: Isaiah 11:1–4; Isaiah 42:1–3; Isaiah 61:1–3, 8–9; Ezekiel 36:24–28; Joel 2:23, 26–30.

The second reading is usually selected from these parts of the New Testament: Acts 1:3–8; Acts 2:1–6,14,22–23,32–33; Acts 8:1,4,14–17; Acts 10:1,33–34,37–44; Acts 19:1–6; Romans 5:1–2,5–8; Romans 8:14–17; Romans 8:26–27.

The Gospel reading is usually selected from: Matthew 5:1–12; Matthew 16:24–27; Matthew 25:14–30; Matthew 1:9–11; Luke 4:16–22; Luke 8:4–10, 11–15; Luke 10:21–24; John 7:37–39; John 14:15–17; John 14:23–26; John 15:18–21,26–27; John 16:5–7,12–13.

By now, you should be familiar with all of them. They are the ones we have been asking you to read and think about during this preparation. In many parishes, the people to be confirmed get to choose the readings they want to use in the celebration. Be prepared to say which ones you would choose and why you would choose them. Also, representatives of the confirmation group are often asked to give the first two readings during the celebration.

Lectionary—
The book used at Mass containing all the readings from Scripture for the various Sundays, feast days, and so forth.

After the readings, you will be officially presented to the celebrant and the community he represents, according to local custom. If your group is small, you will all probably be called by name. If the group is large, you might be called as a group to go up to the celebrant. Basically, this means you become visible. You are showing that you want to answer the call of God and that you are willing to publicly declare yourself a follower of Jesus.

Then the celebrant gives a short homily, or sermon. Listen carefully, because it is not your regular Sunday experience. It will contain many ideas just for you. Remember about being in touch?

Your Turn

When you were just a baby—assuming you were baptized when you were a baby—your parents and godparents said some pretty serious things for you. They promised to share their own faith with you. Now it is your turn. You get the chance to accept or reject what your parents tried to share. The celebrant will now ask you some questions. The expected answer is included. But think about it. Do you really know to what you are saying, "I do"? Do you really want to say "I do"? The choice is yours now. No one has the right to make it for you. No one can make it for you.

Renewal of Baptismal Promises

After the homily, the candidates stand and the bishop questions them:

Bishop:	Do you reject Satan, and all his works, and all his empty promises?
Candidates:	I do.
Bishop:	Do you believe in God, the Father almighty, Creator of heaven and earth?
Candidates:	I do.
Bishop:	Do you believe in Jesus Christ, His only Son, our Lord, who was born of the Virgin Mary, was crucified, died, and was buried, rose from the dead, and is now seated at the right hand of the Father?

Candidates: I do.

Bishop: Do you believe in the Holy Spirit,
the Lord, the giver of life,
who came upon the apostles at Pentecost
and today is given to you sacramentally in confirmation?

Candidates: I do.

Bishop: Do you believe in the holy Catholic Church,
the communion of saints, the forgiveness of sins,
the resurrection of the body, and life everlasting?

Candidates: I do.

The bishop accepts their profession of faith by proclaiming the faith of the Church:

This is our faith. This is the faith of the Church.

We are proud to profess it in Christ Jesus our Lord.

The whole congregation responds:
Amen.

When we say *Amen* at the end of a prayer, it means we are in full agreement with what the prayer said.

Pentecost!

The celebrant now does for you what the apostles did to their first converts. It is what the Church has been doing since the first Pentecost. He will lay his hands upon your head. In a sense, it is your Pentecost. Through his hands you will receive the Spirit of the community he represents. You will receive in a deeper and formal way the Spirit of Jesus and become a full member of that community where Jesus' Spirit dwells.

Before the celebrant does this, he will say:

My dear friends, in baptism God our Father gave the new birth of eternal life to his chosen sons and daughters. Let us pray to our Father that he will pour out the Holy Spirit to strengthen his sons and daughters with his gifts and anoint them to be more like Christ the Son of God.

All pray in silence for a short time.

After he has laid his hands on all of your group, he will pray:

All-powerful God, Father of our Lord Jesus Christ, by water and the Holy Spirit you freed your sons and daughters from sin and gave them new life. Send your Holy Spirit upon them to be their helper and guide. Give them the spirit of wisdom and understanding, the spirit of right judgment and courage, the spirit of knowledge and reverence. Fill them with the spirit of wonder and awe in your presence. We ask this through Christ our Lord.

Amen.

Sacramentary—
The other book used at Mass and other liturgical services that contains the official prayers and rituals to be used.

God's Seal

In ancient times, official messages were sealed. Hot wax was placed on the folded message. To open it you would have had to break the wax. Before the wax got hard, someone would impress the king's seal on the wax. It was usually done with a ring that had the king's sign carved into it. We still have signet rings as jewelry today. The impression in the wax showed that the king owned the message. It was his property. It was official.

After the celebrant lays hands upon you, he will anoint you with oil, making a sign of the cross on your forehead. The cross is God's sign and the celebrant will say these words while he signs you:

N., be sealed with the Gift of the Holy Spirit.

Your "Amen" is your "yes."

This means you are now signed and sealed as God's own special possession, a child of God. The real seal you receive is the Spirit. The Spirit in you is the real proof you are of God, you belong to God, you are possessed by God.

Being claimed by God as one of His special creatures is quite an honor. Carrying God's seal is also a real responsibility.

Peace Be with You

This ancient greeting was used by the first Christians as we say "hello" and "good-bye" today. Each wished the other the peace of Christ's Spirit. It was often joined with a warm handshake or embrace or a kiss. The celebrant now greets all of the newly confirmed by saying:

Peace be with you.

It is a sign of welcome. In the name of the whole Church, he is welcoming you into the community. You respond with the words:

And also with you.

(May you also enjoy the peace of Christ.)

***Amen* is a Hebrew word that means "I believe this with my whole heart" or "I agree completely."**

Prayers of Petition

After you have been welcomed into the community, the ceremony continues with a series of petitions as in a regular Mass. In many parishes, the people being confirmed are asked to help prepare these petitions and pray them for the community. What would your group want to pray for if you are asked to do this?

Next

If the ceremony takes place as part of Mass, everything now proceeds in the regular way with the Preparation of the Gifts and so forth. If it is not a Mass, the celebrant then leads the community in the Lord's Prayer which looks forward to the Eucharistic sharing of the Bread of Life which will take place the next time the community gathers for the Eucharist.

Finally, after the *Our Father* or at the end of the Mass, the celebrant gives one of these two beautiful blessings to all of the community:

Bow your heads and pray for God's blessing.

The bishop extends his hands over the people and sings or says:

God our Father
made you his children by water and the Holy Spirit:
may he bless you
and watch over you with his fatherly love.
Amen.

Jesus Christ the Son of God
promised that the Spirit of truth
would be with his Church forever:
may he bless you and give you courage
in professing the true faith.
Amen.

The Holy Spirit
came down upon the disciples
and set their hearts on fire with love:
may he bless you,
keep you in faith and love,
and bring you to the joy of God's kingdom.
Amen.

The bishop adds immediately:

And may almighty God bless you,
the Father, and the Son, + and the Holy Spirit.
Amen.

Or

Bow your heads and pray for God's blessing.

The bishop extends his hands over the people and sings or says:

God our Father,
complete the work you have begun
and keep the gifts of your Holy Spirit
active in the hearts of your people.
Make them ready to live his Gospel
and eager to do his will.
May they never be ashamed
to proclaim to all the world Christ crucified
living and reigning for ever and ever.
Amen.

The bishop adds immediately:

And may the blessing of almighty God,
the Father, and the Son, + and the Holy Spirit,
come upon you and remain with you forever.
Amen.

With that, the ceremony ends. Your initiation into the community where Jesus and his Spirit dwell is completed. Your new life in the Spirit begins and the whole Church is enriched by your presence. Congratulations and welcome!

Summary

The tradition of being helped by a sponsor as you prepare for your confirmation goes back to the earliest times in the Church. You should choose your sponsor wisely, looking for a mature Christian who can help you prepare for and then live out your confirmation commitment to follow Jesus as a member of the Church. You should choose your confirmation name carefully, too, because it is supposed to have a special religious meaning for you.

The celebration of the Sacrament of Confirmation has three basic parts: a renewal of your baptismal promises; your confirmation rite; and a Eucharist or a ceremony somewhat related to the Eucharist. In that way, all three dimensions of your initiation into the Church (Baptism/Confirmation/Eucharist) are present. The Rite of Confirmation itself includes special prayers, the laying on of hands, anointing with oil, and the sign of peace.

Chapter 8: Activities

Activity 1

Here is a list of some of the things your sponsor should be able to help you do. Put an *X* in front of each one where you would like to have your sponsor's help. Put an O in front of each one where you feel you are all right.

____ Help in learning how to pray

____ Help in learning more about the parish

____ Help in learning how to witness

____ Help in learning how to participate in parish life

____ Help in learning about my faith

____ Help in doing my service project

____ Help in overcoming bad habits and attitudes

____ Help in learning how to recognize the Spirit's action in my life

____ Help in keeping my commitment to the Church

Now write a practice letter to your chosen sponsor in which you include these two things:

a. I chose you as my sponsor because. . . .

b. As my sponsor I am asking you to help me because. . . .

When you have it in the form in which you want it, give it to or mail it to your chosen sponsor.

P.S. Today it is the custom for the sponsor to give you a gift. In an earlier time, it was the custom for you to give the sponsor a gift. Think about it. It is still a good idea.

Activity 2

In the other chapters, you were asked to read and think about many Scripture passages. They are taken from the suggested passages to be used at your confirmation ceremony. They are also listed in this chapter.

Review them and make your own choices of which ones mean the most to you right now.

1. From the Old Testament ______________________________
   Why?

2. From Acts or the Epistles ______________________________
   Why?

3. From the Gospels ______________________________
   Why?

If you could choose any other part of the Bible as a reading in your ceremony instead of the above, what would it be? ______________________________

Why?

Activity 3

In most of the other chapters, you were asked to read Scripture passages and then write down the key things it said about the Spirit of God or about what happens to a person who lives by the Spirit of God.

Now try to pull them together. Use them for your personal final exam before your confirmation. Choose one of these activities:

1. Write a short "epistle" to send to an imaginary friend. In it, you describe God's Spirit and what kinds of things you can do if you really let God's Spirit into your own life.
2. Design a banner you would be willing to help make that could be used as a decoration at your confirmation ceremony. It should symbolize who the Spirit is and what the Spirit enables you to do after being confirmed into the community where the Spirit dwells.
3. Prepare the outline of the homily you could give at your confirmation if you could give it.
4. Prepare your own Prayer of the Faithful that would include what you hope would happen to your class because of confirmation. (Prayer of the Faithful should also be universal: pope, political leaders, and the poor.)
5. Find and copy the words to six hymns or popular songs (you do not need all the verses) that express for you some of the qualities of God's Spirit and or what happens if you live by God's Spirit.

Appendix

The Church Prays

As a confirmed member of the Catholic community, the following prayers and information will be helpful to you.

Praying

Praying is being aware of God's presence and responding to it. There are many ways to pray.

Liturgical Prayer is participating in the worship of the Church, in particular, the Eucharist and the sacraments. It is responding to God as a community while God offers Himself to us.

Individual Prayer is responding to God as an individual. It is a person's own unique response.

Formal Prayer is a response that has been composed by others for persons to use in prayer.

Spontaneous Prayer is a response in which the person praying uses unprepared words that come at the moment.

Expressive Prayer is responding to God in a bodily way. It can include singing, dancing, movement, gestures, or creating art.

Contemplative Prayer is the response to God's presence that happens within a person when that person is alone with God and experiences God's presence, sometimes beyond words in simple holy silence.

There is a place for all kinds of prayer in our lives. How many ways have you prayed?

How to Pray Using Scripture

1. Choose a Gospel passage (use the Sunday Gospel, for example.) Read the passage thoughtfully.
2. Replay the Gospel story in your imagination, placing yourself in the story.
3. Be aware of how you feel about what is happening. Think about what you would say and do.
4. Now tell Jesus or the Father how you feel and what you think about the Gospel story.
5. Before ending your prayer, thank God for something that your prayer made you aware of.

The Lord's Prayer

Our Father, who art in heaven,
Hallowed be thy name,
Thy kingdom come,
Thy will be done on earth as it is in heaven,
Give us this day our daily bread,
And forgive us our trespasses
As we forgive those who trespass against us:
And lead us not into temptation,
But deliver us from evil. Amen.

The Hail Mary

Hail Mary, full of Grace,
The Lord is with you!
Blessed are you among women,
And blessed is the fruit of your womb, Jesus.
Holy Mary, Mother of God,
Pray for us sinners,
Now and at the hour of our death. Amen.

The Trinity Prayer

Glory to the Father, and to the Son, and to the Holy Spirit, as it was in the beginning, is now, and will be forever. Amen.

The Act of Contrition

My God,
I am sorry for my sins with all my heart,
In choosing to do wrong, and failing to do good, I have sinned against You whom I should love above all things.
I firmly intend, with your help, to do penance, to sin no more,
And to avoid whatever leads me to sin.
Our savior, Jesus Christ, suffered and died for us.
In his name, my God, have mercy.

The Apostles' Creed

I believe in God, the Father Almighty, Creator of heaven and earth and in Jesus Christ, His only Son, our Lord, who was conceived by the Holy Spirit, born of the Virgin Mary, suffered under Pontius Pilate, was crucified, died and was buried.

He descended into hell, the third day he arose again from the dead;

he ascended into heaven, sits at the right hand of God, the Father almighty; from thence he shall come to judge the living and the dead.

I believe in the Holy Spirit, the holy Catholic Church, the communion of saints, the forgiveness of sins, the resurrection of the body, and life everlasting. Amen.

Nicene Creed

We believe in one God, the Father, the Almighty, maker of heaven and earth, and all that is seen and unseen.

We believe in one Lord, Jesus Christ, the only Son of God, eternally begotten of the Father, God from God, Light from Light, true God from true God, begotten, not made, one in Being with the Father.

Through him all things were made. For us men and for our salvation he came down from heaven: by the power of the Holy Spirit he was born of the Virgin Mary, and became man. For our sake he was crucified under Pontius Pilate; he suffered, died, and was buried.

On the third day he rose again in fulfillment of the Scriptures; he ascended into heaven and is seated at the right hand of the Father. He will come again in glory to judge the living and the dead, and his kingdom will have no end.

We believe in the Holy Spirit, the Lord, the giver of life, who proceeds from the Father and the Son. With the Father and the Son he is worshiped and glorified. He has spoken through the Prophets. We believe in one holy catholic and apostolic Church. We acknowledge one baptism for the forgiveness of sins. We look for the resurrection of the dead, and the life of the world to come. Amen.

Prayer to the Holy Spirit

Come, Holy Spirit, fill the hearts of your faithful, and enkindle in them the fire of your love. Send forth your spirit and they shall be created. And you shall renew the face of the earth.

O God, who by the light of the Holy Spirit did instruct the hearts of the faithful, grant that by the same Holy Spirit we may be truly wise and ever rejoice in his consolation, through Christ, our Lord. Amen.

Act of Faith

Lord God, I believe that you are one God in three Persons. I believe that you are Father, Son and Holy Spirit. I believe that a new life opened for me through the death and resurrection of your Son and that your love and guidance continue through your Holy Spirit. I believe in the truths taught by your holy, catholic, and apostolic Church. By responding in love to your gifts, I believe that I shall share in eternal joy with you. This is my belief, Lord God, and my belief is my joy. Amen.

Act of Hope

Lord God, trusting in your deep love and goodness, I hope to receive continued forgiveness for my faults and your guidance and help in avoiding sin. My hope for eternal life and joy with you fills me with joy and love each day I live. Amen.

Act of Love

Lord God, you continually share your great love with me through the gifts in my life. In an attempt to imitate your great goodness and show my love in return, I will strive to love you with all my heart, all my mind, and all my strength, and I will seek to love my neighbor as myself. Lord, teach me to love even more. Amen.

The Confiteor

I confess to Almighty God, and to you, my brothers and sisters, that I have sinned through my own fault in my thoughts and in my words, in what I have done and in what I have failed to do; and I ask Blessed Mary, ever Virgin, all the angels and saints, and you, my brothers and sisters, to pray for me to the Lord our God.

Gloria

Glory to God in the highest, and peace to his people on earth.

Lord God, heavenly King, almighty God and Father, we worship you, we give you thanks, we praise you for your glory.

Lord Jesus Christ, only Son of the Father, Lord God, Lamb of God, you take away the sin of the world: have mercy on us;

you are seated at the right hand of the Father: receive our prayer.

For you alone are the Holy One, you alone are the Lord, you alone are the Most High, Jesus Christ, with the Holy Spirit, in the glory of God the Father. Amen.

Divine Praises

Blessed be God.
Blessed be his Holy Name.
Blessed be Jesus Christ, true God and true man.
Blessed be the name of Jesus.
Blessed be his most Sacred Heart.
Blessed be his most precious blood.
Blessed be Jesus in the most holy sacrament of the altar.
Blessed be the Holy Spirit, the Paraclete.
Blessed be the great Mother of God, Mary most holy.
Blessed be her holy and immaculate conception.
Blessed be her glorious assumption.
Blessed be the name of Mary, Virgin and Mother.
Blessed be St. Joseph, her most chaste spouse.
Blessed be God in his angels and in his saints.

Prayer for the Dead

Eternal rest grant unto them, O Lord, and let perpetual light shine upon them. May they rest in peace. Amen.

Serenity Prayer

God grant me the serenity to accept the things I cannot change,
Courage to change the things I can,
And wisdom to know the difference.

Memorare

Remember, O most gracious Virgin Mary, that never was it known that anyone who fled to your protection, implored your help, or sought your intercession was left unaided. Inspired by this confidence, I fly unto you, O Virgin of virgins, my Mother; to you I come, before you I stand, sinful and sorrowful. O Mother of the Word incarnate, despise not my petitions, but in your mercy hear and answer me. Amen. (St. Bernard)

The Magnificat

My soul proclaims the greatness of the Lord, my spirit rejoices in God my Savior for he has looked with favor on his lowly servant.

From this day, all generations will call me blessed; the Almighty has done great things for me. His name is holy; from one generation to another he shows mercy to those who honor him.

He has stretched out his mighty arm and scattered the proud with all their plans. He has brought down mighty kings from their thrones and lifted up the lowly. He has filled the hungry with good things and sent the rich away with empty hands. He has kept the promise he made to our ancestors, and has come to the help of his servant Israel. He has remembered to show mercy to Abraham and to all his descendants forever! (Luke 1:46–55)

Hail, Holy Queen

Hail holy queen, mother of mercy; hail our life, our sweetness, and our hope! To thee do we cry, poor banished children of Eve. To thee do we send up our sighs, mourning and weeping in this vale of tears. Turn then, most gracious advocate, thine eyes of mercy toward us; and after this our exile, show unto us the blessed fruit of thy womb, Jesus.

The Angelus

The angel of the Lord declared to Mary.
And she conceived of the Holy Spirit.
Hail Mary. . . .

Behold the handmaid of the Lord.
Be it done unto me according to your word.
Hail Mary. . . .

And the Word was made flesh,
and dwelt among us.
Hail Mary. . . .

Pray for us, O holy Mother of God.
That we may be made worthy of the promises of Christ.

Let us pray:
Pour forth we beseech you, O Lord, your grace into our hearts that we, to whom the incarnation of Christ, your Son, was made known by the message of an angel, may by his passion and cross be brought to the glory of his resurrection, through the same Christ, our Lord. Amen.

Prayer to St. Joseph

O Joseph, model of all who labor, pray to God with us. It is an honor to use the gifts and develop the talents he has given us. May God's grace strengthen us to work with order and patience, thankfulness and joy. We pray that we may strive dutifully and conscientiously to fulfill our tasks, that all our accomplishments may benefit others and serve their needs. Then may the Lord crown our efforts at the hour of death, that we may join in praising him forever. Amen.

Prayer of St. Francis

Lord, make me an instrument of your peace.
Where there is hatred, let me sow love;
where there is injury, pardon;
where there is doubt, faith;
where there is despair, hope;
where there is darkness, light;
where there is sadness, joy.

O Divine Master, grant that I may not
so much seek to be consoled, as to console;
to be understood, as to understand;
to be loved, as to love.
For it is in giving that we receive;
it is in pardoning that we are pardoned;
and it is in dying that we are born to eternal life.

Examination of Conscience

How did I show my love for God and others?
Did I usually say my daily prayers?
Did I always obey my parents?
Did I think of others—my parents, brothers and sisters, friends? Was I mean to them?
Did I treat my body and that of others with the proper respect?
Was I kind and fair in the way I played and worked?
Did I share my things with others?
Did I care for my things and the things of others?
Did I hurt others by telling lies or by stealing or by calling them names?
Did I worship God by going to Mass and taking part in the celebration?

Mass Responses

Introductory Rite

Priest: The Lord be with you.

People: And also with you.

Penitential Rite

Priest: Brothers and sisters, to prepare ourselves to celebrate the sacred mysteries, let us call to mind our sins.

Priest: You were called to heal the contrite, Lord, have mercy.

People: Lord, have mercy.

Priest: You came to call sinners, Christ have mercy.

People: Christ, have mercy.

Priest: You plead for us at the right hand of the Father, Lord have mercy.

People: Lord, have mercy.

Gospel Response

Priest: This is the Gospel of the Lord.

People: Praise to you, Lord Jesus Christ.

Eucharistic Acclamations

Priest: Let us proclaim the mystery of faith.

People: Christ has died, Christ is risen, Christ will come again.

People: Dying you destroyed our death, rising you restored our life. Lord Jesus, come in glory.

People: When we eat this bread, and drink this cup, we proclaim your death, Lord Jesus, until you come in glory.

People: Lord, by your cross and resurrection you have set us free. You are the Savior of the world.

Rite of Communion

Priest: This is the Lamb of God who takes away the sins of the world. Happy are those who are called to his supper.

People: Lord, I am not worthy to receive you, but only say the word and I shall be healed.

Dismissal

Priest: Go in peace to love and serve the Lord.

People: Thanks be to God.

Stations of the Cross

First Station: Jesus is condemned to death.

Second Station: Jesus is made to carry his cross.

Third Station: Jesus falls the first time.

Fourth Station: Jesus meets Mary, his mother.

Fifth Station: Simon, the Cyrenian, helps Jesus carry his cross.

Sixth Station: Veronica wipes the face of Jesus.

Seventh Station: Jesus falls the second time.

Eighth Station: Jesus speaks to the daughters of Jerusalem.

Ninth Station: Jesus falls the third time.

Tenth Station: Jesus is stripped of his garments.

Eleventh Station: Jesus is nailed to the cross.

Twelfth Station: Jesus dies on the cross.

Thirteenth Station: Jesus is taken down from the cross.

Fourteenth Station: Jesus is laid in the tomb.

The Rosary

The Joyful Mysteries

(Mondays and Thursdays)

The Annunciation

The Visitation

The Birth of Jesus

The Presentation in the Temple

Mary and Joseph Find Jesus in the Temple

The Sorrowful Mysteries

(Tuesdays and Fridays)

The Agony in the Garden

The Scourging of Jesus

The Crowning with Thorns

Jesus Carries his Cross

Jesus Dies on the Cross

The Glorious Mysteries

(Sundays, Wednesdays, and Saturdays)

The Resurrection

The Ascension

The Holy Spirit is Sent upon the Apostles

The Assumption of Mary

Mary Is Crowned Queen of Heaven and Earth

Rules the Church Lives By

The Great Commandments

Love the Lord your God
with all your heart,
with all your soul,
with all your strength,
with all your mind;
and love your neighbor as you love yourself.
(Luke 10:27; Deuteronomy 6:5; Leviticus 19:18)

Jesus' Law of Love

Love one another just as I have loved you.
(John 15:12)

The Ten Commandments

1. I the Lord, am your God. You shall not have other gods besides me.
2. You shall not take the name of the Lord, your God, in vain.
3. Remember to keep holy the Sabbath Day.
4. Honor your father and your mother.
5. You shall not kill.
6. You shall not commit adultery.
7. You shall not steal.
8. You shall not bear false witness against your neighbor.
9. You shall not covet your neighbor's wife.
10. You shall not covet anything that belongs to your neighbor.

(*Sharing the Light of Faith*, National Catechetical Directory, Appendix A)

The Beatitudes

Happy are the poor of spirit;
theirs is the kingdom of God.
Happy are the meek;
they shall inherit the earth.
Happy are those that mourn;
they shall be comforted.
Happy are those who hunger and thirst for justice;
they shall be satisfied.
Happy are the merciful;
they shall have mercy shown to them.
Happy are the pure of heart;
they shall see God.
Happy are the peacemakers;
they shall be called God's children.
Happy are those who are persecuted in the cause of justice;
theirs is the kingdom of God.

Corporal Works of Mercy

Feed the hungry.
Give drink to the thirsty.
Clothe the naked.
Visit the imprisoned.
Shelter the homeless.
Visit the sick.
Bury the dead.

Spiritual Works of Mercy

Convert the sinner.
Instruct the ignorant.
Counsel the doubtful.
Comfort the sorrowful.
Bear wrongs patiently.
Forgive all injuries.
Pray for the living and the dead.

The Laws of the Church

1. To keep Sundays holy; and to participate in Mass on Sunday and holy days of obligation.
2. To lead a sacramental life, frequently receiving the Eucharist.
3. To prepare for confirmation to be confirmed.
4. To observe the marriage laws of the Church and to provide children with religious training.
5. To strengthen and support the Church.
6. To do penance, including abstaining from meat and fasting from food on appointed days.
7. To join in the missionary spirit and works of the Church.

(Adapted from *Concise Catholic Dictionary for Parents and Religion Teachers* by Reynolds Ekstrom and Rosemary Ekstrom)

Holy Days of Obligation

All Catholics everywhere are obliged to observe Christ's passover from death to life by attending the Eucharist on the first day of the week, the Lord's Day or Sunday. The Sunday obligation may be fulfilled on Saturday evening.

In addition, in the United States, the following holy days of obligation are observed:

Christmas (December 25)
The Solemnity of Mary Mother of God (January 1)
Ascension Thursday (fortieth day after Easter)
Assumption of Mary (August 15)
All Saints (November 1)
Immaculate Conception (December 8)

Eucharistic Fast

No food or liquid (except water) is to be taken one hour before receiving Holy Communion.

Days of Penance

All Christ's faithful are obliged by Divine Law, each in his or her own way, to do penance. However, so that all may be joined together in a certain common practice of penance, days of penance are prescribed. On these days, the faithful are in a special manner to devote themselves to prayer, to engage in works of piety and charity, and to deny themselves by fulfilling their obligations more faithfully and especially by observing the fast and abstinence that the following canons prescribe.

The days and times of penance for the universal Church are each Friday of the whole year and the season of Lent.

Abstinence and fasting are to be observed on Ash Wednesday and Good Friday.

The law of abstinence binds those who have completed their fourteenth year. The law of fasting binds those who have attained their majority, until the beginning of their sixtieth year. (The Code of Canon Law, canons 1249–1253)

Catholics in the United States are obliged to abstain from the eating of meat on Ash Wednesday and on all Fridays during the season of Lent. They are also obliged to fast on Ash Wednesday and on Good Friday. Self-imposed observance of fasting on all weekdays of Lent is strongly recommended. Abstinence from flesh meat on all Fridays of the year is especially recommended to individuals and to the Catholic community as a whole.

Glossary

• **Adolescence**

A period of transition between childhood and adulthood.

• **Amen**

A Hebrew word that means "I believe this with my whole heart" or "I agree completely."

• **Beatitudes**

The standards for a happy life given by Jesus in his Sermon on the Mount. (Matthew 5:3–10)

• **Biological Adulthood**

The capacity to reproduce the species.

• **Cardinal (or Moral) Virtues**

prudence, justice, temperance, and fortitude

• **Catechesis**

Comes from the Greek word meaning "to echo." A catechist is also called a religion teacher today. The task of the catechist is to "echo" the truth Jesus taught and to nurture others' faith in Jesus and that truth.

• **Catechumenate**

The official process for preparing new converts for their initiation into the Church. A convert enrolled in the process is called a *catechumen.*

• **Charismatic**

Gifted by the Holy Spirit; devoted to seeking and experiencing special gifts of the Holy Spirit. It is from the Greek word, *charisma,* meaning "gift or favor."

• **Chrism**

Perfumed oil or ointment. It comes from the Greek word for oil. It is root for Christ—the Anointed One—and for Christian—a follower of Christ.

• **Communion of Saints**

The community of both the living members of the Church and all those faithful members of the Church who have lived before us.

• **Community**

People who share something in common and who are bound to each other by what they share.

• **Confirmation**

A sacrament through which those who have been baptized in Christ share more fully in the gifts of the Holy Spirit and in membership in Christ's Church.

• **Conversion**

To change from one religion or set of beliefs to another. But, more fundamentally, it means to turn one's whole self around to God, to change one's heart and be "reborn," to try to grow spiritually. In this sense, we are all called to ongoing conversion as disciples of Jesus.

• **Corporal Works of Mercy**

Human actions, motivated by love of God and neighbor, relating to the bodily needs of others.

• **Crosier**

The staff carried by a bishop. It is modeled after the shepherd's staff with a hook at one end.

• **Cultural Adulthood**

The capacity to form, feed, and care for a family in the society in which you live.

• **Deacon**

Comes from the Greek word, *diakonia,* meaning "service." A deacon is a servant. You can read how the Church first called forth deacons in Acts 6:1–7.

• **Diocese**

An area or district of the Church a bishop governs. The bishop is ultimately responsible for the guidance of all the parishes and all the Catholics in his diocese. The word comes from two Greek words meaning "to keep house" or "to govern a household."

• **Evangelization**

Comes from the Greek word *evangel,* meaning "messenger, an announcer of good news." An evangelist is a messenger sent to tell people the Good News of God's salvation in Jesus and the coming of God's Reign. Evangelization is a primary ministry of the Church.

• **Faith**

To believe in God and the truths revealed by God; one of the theological virtues; "to be sure of the things we hope for, to be certain of the things we cannot see." (Hebrews 11:1)

• **Fear of the Lord**

Great love and reverence for the Lord.

• **Fortitude**

Courage in facing hardship for what is right; one of the cardinal moral virtues.

• **Fruits of the Spirit**

Love, joy, peace, patience, kindness, goodness, faithfulness, humility, and self-control. (Galatians 5:22–23)

• **Fundamentalist**

One who believes in only a literal interpretation of the Bible.

• **Gifts of the Spirit**

Special powers of the Spirit bestowed on the Church and all its members to enable them to carry out Jesus' mission: wisdom, understanding, counsel, fortitude, knowledge, piety, and fear of the Lord.

• **Grace**

God's life within us.

• **Holy Days of Obligation**

Days on which Catholics are required to participate in the Mass.

• **Holy Spirit**

Third Person of the Blessed Trinity; the Spirit of Love.

• **Hope**

The theological virtue that helps us trust in God and His promise of eternal life.

• **Infinite**

To be totally without limits of any kind. Only God is truly infinite.

• **Jesus' Law of Love**

The words of Jesus that sum up all of God's laws: "Love one another just as I love you."

• **Justice**

Giving to people what is rightfully theirs; one of the cardinal moral virtues.

• **Kingdom of God**

The reign of God; everyone can cooperate with God's building of His kingdom by doing God's will.

• **Koinonia**

Greek word for community.

• **Lectionary**

The book used at Mass containing all the readings from Scripture for the various Sundays and feast days.

• **Lent**

The forty-day period of prayer and fasting before Easter, beginning on Ash Wednesday. The season when we prepare to celebrate the mystery of Jesus' death and resurrection and deepen the conversion symbolized and begun in our baptism. The time of final preparation for new converts before they are initiated into the Church at the Easter Vigil.

• **Martyr**

One who sacrifices his or her life for a cause.

• **Mesiah**

Means "anointed one."

• **Minister**

Comes from the Latin for little or less. In the spirit of the Gospel, a minister is supposed to be less than others, that is, a servant to others.

• **Miter**

The tall hat worn by a bishop at official ceremonies. It is a symbol of a bishop's responsibility to serve as a leader in the Church, as the first apostles did.

• **Moral (or Cardinal) Virtues**

prudence, justice, temperance, and fortitude

• **Obligation**

Duties imposed by the laws of God, the Church, or moral law.

• **Occasion of Sin**

Any person, place, or thing that is a temptation to sin for a particular person.

• **Pagan**

Term used to describe anyone who does not believe in God as revealed in the Scriptures—a heathen, an irreligious person.

• **Parapsychology**

The science that studies the mind's ability to act outside the laws of space, time, and matter.

- **Paschal Mystery**

The term used to describe God's plan and action to rescue humanity from sin and death and restore us to fullness of life and holiness in Jesus. Christ's passover from death to life through His saving passion, death, and resurrection.

- **Pastoral Ministry**

Comes from the Latin word for shepherd. A person engaged in pastoral ministry cares for, guides, heals, and protects the members of the Church in the name of Jesus, the Good Shepherd. (Read John 21:15–17.)

- **Pentecost**

Christian feast celebrated fifty days after Jesus' resurrection to remember the outpouring of the Holy Spirit upon Jesus' first followers.

- **People of God**

the Church

- **Precepts of the Church**

Seven Church laws governing Catholics.

- **Prophet**

Comes from the Greek word meaning "to speak out." The ministry of the prophet is to speak out. By speaking out, the prophet tries to help people recognize the action of the Holy Spirit in their lives. The prophet also helps people recognize and turn from the influence of the spirit of the world.

- **Prophecy**

Divine revelation given by God through a person God inspired.

- **Prudence**

A virtue that helps us make practical decisions and judgments; one of the cardinal moral virtues.

- **Rite of Christian Initiation of Adults**

The process by which adults are formally brought into Christ and the Church.

- **Ruah**

The word the Hebrews used for Spirit until almost the time of Jesus.

- **Sacramentary**

Book used at Mass and other liturgical services that contains the official prayer and rituals to be used.

- **Sacraments**

Effective, sacred signs (rites using special words, gestures, and symbols) instituted by Jesus and enacted by the Church through which we experience the saving, healing, and empowering presence and action of Jesus. There are seven Sacraments in the Church.

- **Sacraments of Healing**

Reconciliation and Anointing of the Sick; sacraments which bring Christ's healing to us.

- **Sacraments of Initiation**

Baptism, Confirmation, and Eucharist; the sacraments by which a person is initiated into the Catholic Church.

- **Sacraments of Service**

Holy Orders and Matrimony; sacraments of commitment.

- **Satanism**

A cult devoted to the worship of Satan. It is growing today, often attracting curious youth who become ensnared and controlled by its leaders. Police in most major cities have special details to keep track of Satanic cults, because they have been known to practice murder and human sacrifice.

- **Spirit**

Any nonmaterial force or energy that is not bound by the laws of matter, space, or time.

- **Spiritual**

Nonmaterial; relating to the soul and to one's relationship to God, who is completely spiritual or nonmaterial.

- **Spiritual Adulthood**

The capacity to act responsibly and respect the rights of others.

- **Spiritual Works of Mercy**

Seven charitable works encouraged by the Church related to the spiritual well-being of others.

- **Sponsor**

A person who undertakes the responsibility to guide a confirmation candidate in the preparation for receiving the sacrament. It is the sponsor's role to present the candidate to the Church at the time of the celebration of the sacrament.

- **Theological Virtues**

faith, hope and charity

- **Trinitarian Life**

The life of the Father, Son, and Holy Spirit.

- **Trinity**

Three Persons in one God.

- **Virtue**

Habitual actions that promote the good of an individual or of society.

- **Vocation**

Call from God to a particular way of life.

- **Wisdom**

A gift of the Holy Spirit that enables us to judge rightly about the things of God and to desire the things of God rather than the things of the world.

- **Witness**

To share the good news of Jesus Christ in word and actions.